101 THINGS
YOU NEED TO
KNOW ABOUT
SUFFRAGETTES

101 THINGS YOU NEED TO KNOW ABOUT SUFFRAGETTES

MAGGIE ANDREWS & JANIS LOMAS

This book is dedicated to the next generation:
Edu, Emily, Erin, Florence, Laura, Lucia, Stanley and Tom.

The future is theirs; may they live up to
the hopes and dreams of the feisty Suffragettes.

First published 2018

The History Press
The Mill, Brimscombe Port
Stroud, Gloucestershire, GL5 2QG
www.thehistorypress.co.uk

British Library Cataloguing in Publication Data.
A catalogue record for this book is available from the British Library.

ISBN 978 0 7509 8884 1

Typesetting and origination by The History Press
Printed and bound in Great Britain by TJ International Ltd

ACKNOWLEDGEMENTS

THIS BOOK HAS BEEN WRITTEN WITH HELP FROM a number of students at the University of Worcester who have helped with the research and writing the entries. They are:

Margaret Adkins; Dan Barker; Jennifer Braithwaite; Kevin Brooke; Nicola Connelly; Chloe Cox; Nathan Giles; Jade Gilks; Patrick Hearn; Ana Iscru; Connor Jones; Dan Jordon; Elspeth King; Victoria Martin; Rose Miller; Chloe Morris; Anna Muggeridge; Linda Pike; Phillip Rose; Darren Taft; Molly Tregellis; Michael Wheatley.

INTRODUCTION

IN VICTORIA GARDENS, IN THE SHADOW OF THE HOUSE of Commons, there is a statue of Emmeline Pankhurst. Many of us have heard about the role she and her three daughters – Christabel, Sylvia and Adela – played in winning the vote for women. The activities of the organisation they started, the Women's Social and Political Union (WSPU), included smashing windows, burning postboxes, demonstrations in Parliament Square, being sent to prison and going on hunger strike.

This book will also show some of the other unexpected, ingenious and inventive activities that took place during their fifteen years of activism, and in a much longer fight for women's political enfranchisement and equality. It was a struggle which involved many organisations, women and events, many less well known today than the Pankhursts remain. Before the Pankhurst family and the WSPU began the agitation for which they became famous, other groups of women had been asking, politely, for the right to vote. Their campaigns lasted almost 100 years, from the first women's petition in 1832 until women finally achieved the vote (on equal terms to men, anyway) in 1928.

Householder women could actually vote locally and stand in local elections, and for school boards, prison boards and as Poor Law Guardians, from as early as the 1870s. As women's rights activist Lydia Becker explained in 1896:

Political freedom begins for women, as it begins for men, with freedom in local government ... There can be no training so excellent for women who may be called upon to vote in parliamentary elections, as the thoughtful and intelligent use of the municipal franchises which they already possess.

Women's involvement in local politics often focused on housing, education, and social and infant welfare. For example, Emma Cons' work as a rent collector gave her first-hand knowledge of the housing conditions of the poor, leading her to found the South London Dwellings Co. to provide affordable housing. In 1889 she became the first female Alderman on a London County Council, alongside Jane Cobden and Lady Sandhurst. She worked tirelessly for women's suffrage, commenting wryly:

It is a bitter experience when one for the first time fully realises that even a long life spent in the service of one's fellow citizens is powerless to blot out the disgrace and crime (in the eyes of the law) of having been born a woman.

However, women could not vote in County Council elections until 1907. Suffragette Elizabeth Garrett Anderson became the first female mayor when she was elected in Aldeburgh, Suffolk, in 1908.

Even as late as 1900, less than 60 per cent of the male population had a vote in Britain. The right to vote was based on property qualifications, which excluded many working-class men. In some of the poorer areas of the country, such as Glasgow, less than half the male population had the franchise. Many Labour Party politicians focused on campaigning to extend the franchise to everybody over the age of twenty-one, and formed the Adult Suffrage Society. The members were known as 'Adultists'. Their president in 1906 was in fact a woman: Margaret Bondfield, a Trades Union campaigner and activist in the Shop Assistants' Union. In January 1929, she was to become the first female Cabinet minister in British history.

Despite years of campaigning by the National Union of Women's Suffrage Societies (NUWSS) and other groups, there was little or no progress towards women's enfranchisement. In 1903, Emmeline Pankhurst and her daughters formed the Women's Social and Political Union (WSPU) in Manchester. They developed innovative tactics to get the issue of women's suffrage onto the front pages of the newspapers. A *Daily Mail* headline writer coined the word Suffragette in 1906, which was frequently, although not exclusively, used to refer to those who were prepared to break the law to pursue their cause. In the Edwardian era a multitude of suffrage groups emerged, including the Artists' Suffrage League (1907), Actresses' Franchise League (1908), the Women Writers' Suffrage League, the Barmaids' Political Defence League, the Gymnastic Teachers' Suffrage Society and the Catholic Women's Suffrage Society.

The first British dominion to give women the vote was the Isle of Man, which enfranchised women in 1881. The Manchester National Society for Women's Suffrage congratulated the women electors of the Isle of Man on being the first women 'within her Majesty's dominions whose rights as parliamentary electors have been legally recognised'. As there were three seats in the House of Keys' parliament and four male candidates, no woman stood for election. Nonetheless, the first person to cast their vote was a woman. In 1893, New Zealand became the first country to enfranchise women, followed by some states in Australia in 1902. Finland, Norway, Denmark, Iceland, USSR and Canada all enfranchised women before Great Britain. The first female MPs in the world were elected in Finland in 1907.

In 1909 the Liberal government introduced a suffrage bill proposing women's suffrage for some women and the vote for virtually all men. The bill initially seemed to progress well but was dropped when an election was called. In the months that followed, Suffragettes' anger at these broken promises led to a campaign that definitely deserved the name 'deeds, not words':

window smashing began in earnest, alongside attacks on public buildings and services. This aggression was not one-sided: the establishment, and the policemen who enforced the status quo, often resorted to terrible violence in their efforts to suppress the women's efforts to win the vote. On 18 November 1910, on what became known as Black Friday, a deputation of women attempted to reach the prime minister to protest about his failure to carry through a bill for women's suffrage. The women were treated appallingly roughly: many were knocked to the ground, others kicked and trampled before they were able to get up. Plain-clothed policemen disguised as working men (and helped by some uniformed officers) carried out assaults on the women. Some of the assaults were of a sexual nature: women complained of hands being thrust up their skirts, and of having their breasts felt and squeezed; one woman described her breasts being wrung painfully, accompanied by the retort, 'You've been wanting this for a long time, haven't you?' Being struck on their breasts was particularly distressing to women, as it was believed at the time to cause breast cancer. As another example, it was reported that Suffragette Mary Frances Earl had her 'undergarments' torn from her by a policeman; he used foul language as he attacked and proceeded to drag her up some steps by her hair. The bravery of the so-called 'weaker sex', who faced such horrors and nonetheless battled determinedly onwards, should never be forgotten.

Many other political groups used violence to articulate political frustration in this era too. Violence was nothing new to Edwardian political life. When Lloyd George endeavored to speak against the Boer War in Birmingham in 1901, for example, 350 policemen were drafted to protect him from the attentions of an estimated 30,000 protestors. The ensuing chaos led to two deaths, including that of a policeman, as well as forty hospital admissions. Campaigns using violence created anxiety within the Westminster establishment, but not all groups were treated the same way. Churchill initially refused to send in army troops to deal with the rioting miners in Tonypandy in 1910, in an attempt to avoid escalating the violence. British authorities were also worried that anarchist ideology from Europe would spread to Britain. They even surrounded one Swiss anarchist-turned-informant in hospital in Tottenham with armed guards. The papers reported fears that other anarchists would 'attack the hospital, blow it up or destroy it with dynamite' to silence him. Opposition to a parliamentary bill to introduce Home Rule in Ireland led, in 1912, to the formation of the Ulster Volunteers, and over 100,000 men joined Edward Carson in signing the Ulster Covenant, which bound its adherents to resist Home Rule for Ireland by 'all means necessary'. Nonetheless, it seems that the violence enacted by the Suffragettes particularly appalled people, as it challenged deeply held ideas of femininity.

All was not sweetness and light in the Suffragette sisterhood itself either; even within the Pankhurst family, there were tensions. Not everyone in the movement agreed with Emmeline and her daughter Christabel's leadership style, nor with their militant tactics. Consequently, a plethora of different suffrage organisations emerged in the run up to the First World War.

By 1912 militancy had escalated to unprecedented levels, moving from attempts to gain public sympathy to coercive tactics; the government responded harshly and public opinion began to turn even more firmly against the militants. Newspapers vilified the Suffragettes and advocated extreme punishments for them. The *Derby Daily Express* declared that every militant Suffragette should have their head shaved and be whipped with the cat-o'-nine tails. As the First World War approached, and violent protests grew, the WSPU began haemorrhaging members. With depleted funds, the WSPU appeared to be running out of steam. On the other hand, membership in the non-violent constitutional group the NUWSS grew during the same period; NUWSS branches expanded from thirty-three in 1907 to 478 by 1912. This growth may, however, have also been boosted by the publicity generated by the militants' actions.

May. 1913

WSPU OFFICE IN 1913. (LSE, 7JCC/O/02/123)

By the end of the First World War in 1918, the Representation of the People Act, which gave some women the vote, was finally on the statute books. It extended the right to vote to about 6 million women aged thirty or over, as long as they met certain property qualifications – in their own right or through their husbands. Munitions workers, who had contributed so much to the war effort, did not generally meet these requirements. Neither did domestic servants. Many suffrage campaigners, including Lilian Lenton, were also indignant that, having suffered so much, they were still deemed too young to exercise a vote. Furthermore, the confusion around who actually had the right to vote was so great that many women who could vote did not. Consequently, the number of women who voted in the 1918 election was disappointingly low.

The struggle for political equality was not over either. It took another ten years for women to be enfranchised on the same terms as men. Nonetheless, in 1918 a victory party was held at the Queen's Hall to celebrate. Blake's poem 'Jerusalem', which had recently been set to music, was chosen as the new anthem for the women's suffrage movement. Women continued to campaign for equal citizenship and suffrage supporters joined a range of new campaigning organisations. The Six Point Group sought legal, political, occupational, moral, social and economic equality for women. The Sexual Qualifications Removal Act in 1919 stated: 'A person shall not be disqualified by sex or marriage from the exercise of any public function, or from being appointed to or holding any civil or judicial office or post.' For the first time, after its passing, women were able to become magistrates and sit on juries.

The continuing opposition to equal rights was led by prominent figures including the prime minister, Lloyd George. Despite this, in 1928 both Houses of Parliament passed the legislation for equal enfranchisement with an overwhelming majority, without objections and with the minimum of comment. Lord Birkenhead wound up the House of Lords' debate by declaring, 'My recommendation to your Lordships is to go into the Lobby in favour of this bill, if without enthusiasm, yet in a spirit of resolute resignation.'

Britain was at least ahead of many of its European neighbours: France did not enfranchise women until 1944, and in Switzerland women only gained the right to vote in federal elections in 1971. (By contrast, in Saudi Arabia women were first allowed to vote in municipal elections in 2015.) However, it was still to take until 1970 for Equal Pay legislation to finally become law. Despite its passing, even today women earn less than men.

This book cannot cover all of the multifarious undertakings and experiences that make up the history of women's fight for the suffrage, but hopefully it provides instead a starting point, for some, and for all a selection of shining examples of the bravery and determination of the women (and men) who fought to change the political landscape of Britain forever.

FEMALE SUFFRAGE CAMPAIGNERS WERE KILLED AT THE PETERLOO MASSACRE

IN AUGUST 1819, THE RADICAL MP HENRY HUNT MADE his way to address a rally at St Peter's Field, Manchester. Bands entertained the crowds, who were peacefully campaigning for parliamentary reform and an end to the system of 'rotten boroughs': sparsely populated regions which were represented by an MP (at great personal benefit to the incumbent) while huge industrial areas, such as Manchester, had hardly any.

Approximately 12 per cent of the 60,000- to 80,000-strong crowd were women. They included a group of suffrage campaigners

CONTEMPORARY PRINT OF THE PETERLOO MASSACRE. (CL/2018)

from the textile mills known as the Manchester Female Reform Society (one of several such groups formed at that time). Dressed in white, the group was led out to the field by their president, Mary Fildes. The peaceful demonstration turned ugly when local magistrates ordered the arrest of Henry Hunt and the other organisers. Soldiers on horseback rode straight into the crowd, deliberately slashing at the densely packed protestors with their sabres (which had been sharpened before the event, to ensure maximum damage was inflicted). Seven men and four women died.

Mary Hayes, a pregnant mother of six, went into premature labour after she was ridden over by the cavalry. She later died. Margaret Downes' death, meanwhile, was caused by a sabre wound. Another woman, Sarah Jones, a mother of seven, died after being beaten around the head with a special constable's truncheon. Richard Carlile, due to address the crowds that day, stated that women were deliberately targeted. The president of the group of mill girls was amongst them: as an eyewitness later described, 'Mrs Fildes was hanging, suspended by a nail on the platform of the carriage, caught by her white dress. She was slashed across her exposed body by an officer of the cavalry.' Mary Fildes, however, recovered from her injuries and continued to campaign for women's suffrage into the 1830s and 1840s.

WOMEN WERE NOT TECHNICALLY BARRED FROM VOTING UNTIL 1832

002

HENRY HUNT (THE MP IN THE PREVIOUS ITEM) PUT forward a bill, proposed by Mary Smith from Yorkshire, specifying that every unmarried female who met a property qualification should be given the vote.

When MPs agreed the wording of the so-called 'Great Reform Act' of 1832, the legislation referred to 'male persons' rather than 'persons', explicitly excluding women from voting for the first time in British history. The Act increased the suffrage from 366,000 to 650,000 men – approximately 18 per cent of the total adult-male population in England and Wales. More male persons were enfranchised in the 1867 and 1884 Reform Acts.

A POLITICAL CARTOON SHOWING HENRY HUNT AND OTHERS CAMPAIGNING IN WESTMINSTER IN 1818. (LIBRARY OF CONGRESS, LC-DIG-DS-01038)

THE FIRST EVER WOMEN'S SUFFRAGE COMMITTEE WAS INSPIRED BY A WALKING TOUR

IN 1850, AGED JUST TWENTY-THREE, BARBARA LEIGH Smith embarked on a walking tour through Europe with a female friend, Bessie Rayner Parkes. Once out of Britain, the pair abandoned their restrictive corsets, and shortened their skirts to make walking easier. Barbara wrote a little ditty at the time expressing the freedom she felt:

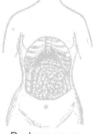

Oh! Isn't it jolly,
To cast away folly,
And cut all one's clothes a peg shorter.
(A good many pegs),
And rejoice in one's legs,
Like a free-minded Albion's daughter.

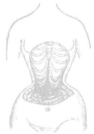

Barbara never wore her corsets again. On returning to England, emboldened by the trip, Barbara began to gather around her a group of like-minded women friends, who all saw education, the right for married women to keep their own earnings and property, employment, and the vote as key to advancing the cause of women. This led to the founding of the Kensington Ladies Discussion Society in 1865, her talk to the group on the subject of women's rights leading to the formation of the first ever Women's Suffrage Committee, with Barbara as its secretary. Barbara toured the country giving speeches, converting many women to the cause of suffrage (including the Manchester suffrage leader Lydia Becker).

SOME WOMEN ACTUALLY VOTED AS EARLY AS 1867

CLERICAL ERRORS MEANT THAT THE FIRST WOMEN to vote did so more than fifty years before universal suffrage became law.

One such woman we know of, Lily Maxwell, was accidentally included on the electoral register in Manchester in 1867. Accompanied by suffrage campaigner Lydia Becker, she therefore came to the polls to cast her vote. 'Woman!!!' is handwritten on the electoral register next to her name. We do not know who wrote this comment, but it was most probably added by the clerk as a result of the publicity generated by her vote.

A month later, in a Manchester by-election, another woman, Jesse Godber, also voted. However, she received little publicity from suffragists, because she decided to cast her vote for an anti-women's suffrage candidate! In 1868, Sarah Ann Jackson summed up the feelings of many women householders with this rhyme:

> I am a working woman,
> My voting half is dead,
> I hold a house and want to know,
> Why I can't vote instead.

It was a question women were to ask over and over in the following decades.

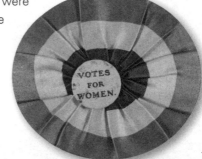

VOTES FOR WOMEN BADGE.
(LSE, 7EWD/M/19A)

MILLICENT GARRETT FAWCETT BECAME A FEMINIST after suffering a distressing inconvenience: her purse was stolen. When she reported the theft to the police, however, she was shocked to discover the thief was charged with 'stealing from the person of Millicent Fawcett a purse containing £1-18-6d, the property of Henry Fawcett'. Henry was her husband. She later recalled that she 'felt as if I had been charged with theft myself'.

She began her long campaigning career by fighting for a change in the law to enable married women to keep their earnings and their own property, which at the time automatically became the property of their husband on marriage. When this fight was finally concluded successfully, in 1882, she moved on to campaigning for the vote. She founded and became the leader of the National Union of Women's Suffrage Society (NUWSS), the largest women's suffrage organisation, in 1897.

Under her guidance, and unlike the members of the rival WSPU, the NUWSS used only legal tactics to fight for enfranchisement. Fawcett herself lived to see women achieve the vote. However, she believed that emancipation was ongoing, each generation required to deal with the grievances of its own time.

MILLICENT FAWCETT WITH OTHER CAMPAIGNERS AT A SUFFRAGE DEMONSTRATION, C. 1920. (LSE, 7JCC/O/02/145)

MILLICENT GARRETT FAWCETT LED THE INVESTIGATION INTO BOER CONCENTRATION CAMPS

IN 1899, THE BRITISH BECAME INVOLVED IN THE SOUTH African War, often known as the Boer War. The British, unable to defeat the Boers' guerrilla tactics, responded by destroying homes and farms, moving thousands of women and children into concentration camps. Emily Hobhouse, a member of the South African Reconciliation Committee (SARC) and the South African Women and Children Distress Fund, published a diary of visits to the camps in the *Manchester Guardian* in 1901:

> Imagine the heat outside the tents and the suffocation inside ... The sun blazed through the single canvas and the flies lay thick and black on everything ... In this tiny tent lives Mrs B's five children (three quite grown up) and a little Kaffir servant girl.

Hobhouse was accused of misunderstanding the Boer way of life, of being hysterical, and of overreacting to wartime conditions. This was not true: these appalling conditions, along with poor organisation and inadequate supplies, brought disease and death to thousands.

Many women involved with suffrage campaigns, both before and during the hostilities, expressed their opposition to the conflict, joining the Stop the War Committee (STWC) and the SARC. Protests against what they described as 'the wicked South African War' included the distribution of anti-war literature in libraries, reading rooms and coffee shops. As an imperialist who supported the war, Mrs Millicent Fawcett, the leader of the NUWSS, therefore found her sentiments at odds with many of her friends. In an attempt to defend her views, Mrs Fawcett suggested that writers like Hobhouse seemed to be collecting information only

MRS FAWCETT IN HYDE PARK IN 1913. (LSE, 7JCC/O/01/177)

from hostile witnesses. In the face of such controversy, the British government appointed Millicent to lead a 'Ladies Commission' to look into the conditions in the camps and to suggest some possible improvements, one of the first occasions in which women had been given such a role in government. The management and the environment in the camps was, by the time the commission arrived, already improving. Nevertheless, the ladies were forced to admit that they generally agreed with Hobhouse's earlier findings.

ONE OF THE FIRST BILLS FOR WOMEN'S SUFFRAGE WAS WRITTEN BY EMMELINE PANKHURST'S HUSBAND

THE FIRST WOMEN'S SUFFRAGE DEBATE CAME MUCH earlier than many people realise: in 1867.

Between 1867 and 1902 around a dozen petitions and resolutions were debated, and three more amendments to Reform Bills were brought forward. Some of these bills, such as the Women's Disabilities Removal Bill, one of the first ever suffrage bills, were written by the Manchester solicitor Richard Marsden Pankhurst. He also drafted the 1882 bill which finally allowed women to retain control over their property after marriage.

Richard was married to Emmeline Pankhurst, twenty-four years his junior. Known as 'the Red Doctor' for his socialist views, Richard shared his wife's view on the rights of women. They also shared an interest in radical politics and took part in a meeting on free speech in Trafalgar Square on 13 November 1887 which had been banned by the Police Commissioner. The clash between police and the public was so violent that it is also known as 'Bloody Sunday'. Richard's unflinching support for women's suffrage lost him many of his most important clients. As a result, at the time of his unexpected death (from gastric ulcers) in July 1898 he left his wife and four young children with little to live on save their debts. Money was to be a continuing worry throughout Emmeline's widowhood: when she died, her estate was worth just £86 5s 6d.

RICHARD PANKHURST. (LSE, 7JCC/0/02/081)

THE SUFFRAGETTES BEGAN THEIR FIGHT IN MANCHESTER

AFTER HER HUSBAND'S DEATH IN 1898, EMMELINE Pankhurst worked as a registrar of births and deaths. This role, along with her work as a member of a school board and as a Poor Law Guardian, gave her experience of working-class women's lives. Then, in 1903, she applied to hold and attend meetings at the newly built Richard Pankhurst Memorial Hall, named after her husband and decorated by her daughter, Sylvia. She was refused. Understandably, she was incensed. This snub was the catalyst for her founding the WSPU.

At the first meeting, held at Emmeline's home in Nelson Street, Manchester, all of the small gathering of women were members of the Independent Labour Party (ILP). Progress was slow: by the summer of 1905, membership was fewer than thirty members. The group moved to London in 1906, where the decision to start carrying out more daring (and publicity-grabbing) protests was taken. Numbers grew rapidly as a result and, by 1910, the group's membership was estimated to be at least 36,000 strong.

EMMELINE PANKHURST IN MANCHESTER. (LSE. 7JCC/O/02/103)

SUFFRAGETTES SOLD THEIR JEWELLERY TO RAISE FUNDS

THE SUFFRAGETTES SUPPORTED THEIR CAUSE IN unusual and clever ways. They harnessed the power of celebrity: best-selling novelist John Galsworthy was one celebrity whose support they drew on, for example; he donated signed copies of his books to be auctioned.

Where money was hard to come by (as was often the case in this era, the finances invariably being in the hands of a husband or a father), they used other resources available to them. For example, Suffragette Hannah Mitchell recalled a meeting in London's Exeter Hall in 1907 where wealthy women removed their jewellery and placed it in the collecting tins. A 'Self Denial Week' was held in February 1908: members did without luxuries such as cocoa, coffee and tea, and donated the resulting savings to the WSPU. By 1910 the WSPU filled Queen's Hall with 2,500 supporters each week, and their annual income had risen to £36,000 (the present-day equivalent is almost £2,376,000), enabling the organisation's London headquarters to grow from two to thirty-seven rooms.

JOHN GALSWORTHY. (LIBRARY OF CONGRESS, LC-USZ62-83088)

23

EMMELINE PANKHURST STARRED IN A MOVIE

MADE IN 1913, *WHAT 80 MILLION WANT* WAS A detective story in which the resourceful heroine, Mabel, supports women's suffrage campaigns, foils would-be assassins and uncovers corrupt politicians, announcing, 'We must fight for right!'

The film features both American suffrage campaigner Harriet Stanton Black (daughter of America's founding suffragist, Elizabeth Cady Stanton), and Mrs Pankhurst herself. Emmeline addresses the crowd in the opening scenes. Given that this was a silent movie, however, the impact of this scene relied less upon her fiery delivery and more upon Emmeline's iconic status. The film, which was directed by Will Louis, written by a female scriptwriter, Florence Maule Cooley, and produced by the Unique Film Company, was approximately an hour long. It was not exactly a blockbuster, but advance notices for the film claimed that 'no more advertised personages can be found to-day than the two militant leaders'.

EMMELINE PANKHURST. (LSE, 7JCC/O/02/087)

CHRISTABEL PANKHURST WAS ARRESTED OUTSIDE A TALK BY WINSTON CHURCHILL

CHRISTABEL PANKHURST AND ANNIE KENNEY GAINED notoriety on Friday, 13 October 1905, after a meeting at The Free Trade Hall, Manchester.

There they challenged and disrupted speeches by Winston Churchill, the second time Christabel had heckled him at a public event. This time Christabel confronted him with the question: 'If you are elected, will you do your best to make Women's Suffrage a government measure?' She then unfurled a Suffragette banner emblazoned with 'votes for women'. This resulted in the pair being ejected from the hall.

They continued their protest outside, until Superintendent Watson demanded that they 'behave as ladies should, and not create any further disturbance'. The ladies were not impressed: during the struggle that followed, Christabel apparently called out, 'I shall assault you!' and later, 'I shall spit at you!' Spitting at a policeman was an offence. Christabel later claimed she had never intended to carry out her threat: expectorating at a policeman was too unlady-like, she insisted, 'even for something as important as the vote'. Nonetheless, the scuffle led to their arrests, Winston expressing the hope that her time in prison 'may soothe her fevered brain'.

ANNIE KENNEY AND CHRISTABEL PANKHURST. (7JCC/O/02/122)

WINSTON CHURCHILL WAS NEARLY KILLED BY SUFFRAGETTES AT A RAILWAY STATION

SUFFRAGETTES OFTEN HECKLED GOVERNMENT ministers and disrupted political meetings with shouted questions about women's suffrage. Flora Drummond targeted Winston Churchill particularly for, as president of the Board of Trade and then Home Secretary, he was a prominent member of a Liberal government that gave little priority to enfranchising women.

Flora, once described in print as a 'pugnacious Scots woman', confronted Churchill on every possible occasion, but she was not the only woman to do so. On 9 November 1909, Theresa Garnett accosted Winston Churchill at Bristol Temple Meads station. She held a horsewhip in her hand. Some reports claimed that, during the scuffle that followed, Churchill nearly fell onto the tracks, and was only saved by his wife grabbing at his coat-tails. Theresa Garnett denied striking Churchill with the whip, but she was convicted of disturbing the peace and imprisoned for

A YOUNG WINSTON CHURCHILL.
(LIBRARY OF CONGRESS, LC-USZ62-65636)

28

a month in Horsfield Jail. She later applied to the courts (unsuccessfully) for the return of her whip!

Churchill's reticence to support the Women's Suffrage Bill in Parliament meant he remained a target of Suffragette anger, exacerbated after Black Friday, when he declared that the Metropolitan Police, whose violence that day is well documented, had 'behaved with forbearance and humanity'. He repudiated 'the unsupported allegations which have issued from that copious fountain of mendacity the WSPU'. Attacks on him continued for several years: in 1910, Kitty Marshall was imprisoned for fourteen days for throwing a potato at the fanlight over Churchill's front door; the following year, Ethel Moorhead threw an egg at him during a political meeting in Dundee. In the same year, 1911, Hugh Franklin, the founder of the Men's Political Union for Women's Enfranchisement, was arrested for hitting Churchill with a dog whip in a railway carriage, shouting, 'Take that, you cur, for the treatment of the suffragists!'

TWO SUFFRAGETTES HAD THEMSELVES POSTED TO THE PRIME MINISTER

SUFFRAGETTES SOUGHT INNOVATIVE WAYS TO petition Parliament and get access to MPs who might aid their cause, designing all their activities to achieve maximum publicity. In October 1908, for example, the women attempted a 'Rush on Parliament'. Labour MP Keir Hardie's secretary, Mrs Travers Symons, actually managed to make it to the floor of the House while a debate was in progress. She was swiftly bundled out again.

In January 1909 two Suffragettes, Daisy Solomon and Elspeth McClelland, came up with one of the most ingenious schemes in British history: they had themselves posted to Prime Minister Asquith from the Strand. At the time, postal law allowed for the delivery of persons on payment of an appropriate fee for stamping (three pennies): Christabel Pankhurst therefore sent the pair to the East Strand Post Office, where they were carefully addressed to 'The Right Hon H. Asquith, 10 Downing Street, SW', and escorted by an official telegraph messenger boy through the police guard and up to the steps of No. 10. Unfortunately, the scheme failed when the Downing Street butler refused to take delivery, declaring them 'dead letters' and thus requiring they be returned to sender.

DAISY SOLOMON AND ELSPETH MCCLELLAND WITH A MESSENGER BOY, POLICE AND AN OFFICIAL OUTSIDE NO. 10 DOWNING STREET, ATTEMPTING TO GET THEMSELVES DELIVERED AS LETTERS. (LSE, 7JCC/O/02/008)

SUFFRAGETTES INVADED PARLIAMENT MORE THAN EIGHTY TIMES

014

THE PARLIAMENTARY ARCHIVES CONTAIN OVER EIGHTY reports of incidents involving Suffragette incursions within the Palace of Westminster between 1906 and the outbreak of the First World War.

Two particularly dramatic incidents occurred on 23 October 1906 and 11 June 1913. On the first, Suffragettes went to the House of Commons. Only thirty women were allowed to enter the lobby but,

once inside, they struggled to get the MPs in attendance to listen to their arguments. Mary Gawthorpe then proceeded to mount a settee next to Lord Northcote's statue and, surrounded by other Suffragettes, attempted to make a speech – only to be removed by police amidst a scuffle.

On the second date, a male suffragist threw a paper bag filled with flour at the prime minister. According to reports circulated as widely as the *LA Herald*, the missile 'missed Asquith and struck the parliamentary clerk full in the face, exploding in a white cloud. The clerk fell to the floor and arose as white as a ghost from head to heel.' An MP rose to protest – and was immediately struck by

MARY GAWTHORPE. (LSE, TWL 2002 47)

a second bomb. A rain of Suffragette pamphlets followed. The thrower, a young man, was eventually captured and thrown out. A member of the East End Federation of Suffragettes was another such flour-bomb thrower. She hid herself inside a large padded box labelled 'CROCKERY: WITH CARE' which was delivered to the House of Commons at night. The next morning, the daring protestor climbed out and secreted herself in the public gallery at the House of Commons, from where she proceeded to fling a 3lb bag of flour at the prime minister. Her aim was better. 'ASQUITH FLOURED ALL OVER' made for an eye-catching newspaper head-line in the following morning's press.

SUFFRAGETTES PRODUCED A COOK BOOK

FOOD WAS AN INTEGRAL ELEMENT OF MANY Suffragette meetings: homes, halls, tea shops and vegetarian restaurants were often accompanied by tea and cake.

Responding to this, Mrs Aubrey Dowson produced *The Suffrage Cookery Book*. It was very popular, and the Women's Printing Society produced several editions. In a format that was also very popular amongst the USA suffrage societies, the book contained recipes sent in by suffrage supporters from across the country, grouped under headings such as 'salads and sauces', 'sweetmeats', and 'bread, cakes, scones and biscuits'. There was a section on vegetarian recipes, including such gems as 'Mrs Impey's King's Norton Rice Cutlets' and 'Savoury Haricot Pie'. The famous Mrs Fawcett provided a recipe for raspberry jam, and Mrs Phillip Snowden donated a recipe for Yorkshire gingerbread; both were prominent members of the NUWSS, and the book's red cover suggests that the funds it raised went to a non-militant section of the movement.

The book also includes a section entitled 'Menus for Busy Suffrage Workers'. This is made up of recipes which can be eaten quickly and will keep hot without spoiling, to accommodate the demands of campaigning. It ends with a slightly tongue-in-cheek entry from Mrs Bertrand Russell: 'Recipe for Cooking and Preserving a Good Suffrage Speaker'. The five suggestions end with: 'Do not let her cool too rapidly after the meeting, but place her considerately by a nice bedroom fire, with a light supper to be taken in solitude.'

MRS HENRY FAWCETT AND MRS PHILIP SNOWDEN,
WHO BOTH CONTRIBUTED RECIPES.

(LSE, 7JCC/O/02/145)

SUFFRAGE RALLIES WERE PICKETED BY THE ANTI-SUFFRAGISTS

THE RIDICULE POURED ON SUPPORTERS OF WOMEN'S suffrage was fierce: examples include the newspaper seller who was recorded calling out 'Votes for women, votes for dogs, votes for donkeys', and a wealthy man, showing off to his friends, who reportedly stuck his head out of his motor-car window and hollered, 'I suppose if you had a vote you would take it home and put it in a mince pie, wouldn't you?' at a passing Suffragette. She had the last word though, replying, 'Perhaps I might do as you do: take it to the Town Hall and make a "hash" of it.'

Despite this public contempt, early rallies were generally peaceful. Women at early WSPU events carried babies, whilst young children walked holding their mother's hands. However, this began to change as the movement began to grow, and police and onlookers became increasingly aggressive. Assaults on Suffragettes grew increasingly commonplace. The women endeavored,

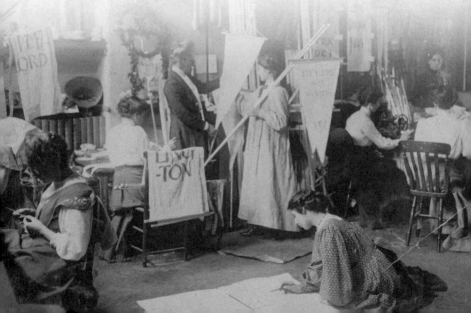

through their dress and demeanor, to convey their respectability. Nevertheless, gangs of men sometimes shouted abuse and threw rotten fruit, stones, dead mice and stink bombs at the women as they marched.

There are also many reports that show that women were physically assaulted as the police stood by. In central Edinburgh in October 1909, for example, a group of young men violently interrupted a suffrage pageant and procession organised by the WSPU; the women carried banners declaring, 'What's good for John is good for Janet', 'Nae gain without pain' and 'To Mr Asquith – Ye mamma tramp on the Scotch thistle laddie'. The picketers did not achieve their aims, highlighting instead the strength of the women's resolve. The *Edinburgh Evening Despatch* reported: 'The imposing display [that is, the women's march] achieved its object. It advertised to tens of thousands the aims of the Suffragettes … Behind this movement there is a solid phalanx of resolute and unflinching womanhood bent upon obtaining the vote and fully determined that they will triumph over every obstacle.'

MAKING BANNERS FOR A 'MAMMOTH PROCESSION OF THE SUFFRAGETTES' ON 23 JULY 1910 (LSE, 7JCC/O/02/015) AND THE SCOTTISH DELEGATION IN 1909. (LSE, 7JCC/O/02/023)

SUFFRAGETTES BARRICADED THEMSELVES INTO HOUSES TO AVOID PAYING TAX

SOME SUFFRAGETTES DECIDED THAT, AS THE government ignored their claim to be citizens and voters, the requirement that they be taxpayers should also be ignored. They therefore refused to pay taxes, and as a result were visited by bailiffs seeking to seize goods in lieu of the unpaid dues. Dora Montefiore, a member of the Practical Suffragists, had her goods seized in 1904 and 1905. By 1906, she was ready: she barricaded herself into her home for several weeks to prevent first the tax collector and then the bailiffs impounding her goods. 'The siege of Fort Montefiore', as the newspapers dubbed it, gained nationwide publicity for the tax issue.

The Women's Tax Resistance League (WTRL) was formed in 1909 with the slogan 'No Vote, No Tax'. 220 women refused to pay their taxes in the five years that the WTRL existed, twenty-three of whom were doctors (including the famous Louisa Garrett Anderson). Other prominent resisters included the Duchess of Bedford and Emmeline's daughter Adela Pankhurst.

SUFFRAGE PARADE IN 1908. (LSE. TWL.1999.250.2)

REPRESENTATION IS TYRANNY

UNIVERSITY GRADUATES PETITIONED FOR THE RIGHT TO VOTE ON THE GROUNDS OF INTELLIGENCE

SUFFRAGETTE CAMPAIGNERS PRODUCED A POSTER portraying a woman university graduate in a gown and mortarboard with the strapline 'Convicts and Lunatics have no vote for Parliament. Should Women be classed with these?'

In June 1906, five Edinburgh University women graduates petitioned the Court of Session for the right to vote for their University MP on the basis of their intellect. Despite two appeals, their gender continued to debar them from the franchise. In November 1908 they took their case to the House of Lords. Although their campaign was ultimately unsuccessful, it was a catalyst for the formation of many university suffrage societies.

(LSE, F35C)

019 SUFFRAGETTES WERE OFTEN TEMPERANCE CAMPAIGNERS TOO

IN THE NINETEENTH CENTURY THE TEMPERANCE movement and the suffrage movement shared friends, money, political affiliations and tactics; both lobbied, gathered signatures and campaigned for sympathetic MPs to be elected. Many Temperance supporters believed alcohol exacerbated working-class poverty and also fuelled the domestic violence that many women suffered.

Lady Isabella Somerset, a keen supporter of women's suffrage in Britain and America, was elected president of the British Women's Temperance Society in the 1890s. Following a most unsatisfactory marriage to the second son of the Duke of Beaufort, who was gay, she proceeded to appall Victorian society by publicly revealing this fact as part of the resulting custody battle over her son. Withdrawing to her family estates in Herefordshire, where her family owned Eastnor Castle, she became increasingly concerned about the effects of alcohol after seeing its impact on the poor families she visited. As a journalist and writer, she promoted her Temperance message through the publication *The Woman's Signal*, encouraging people to take the Total Abstinence Pledge. She became president of the World's Women's Christian Temperance Association in the twentieth century, when she also ran the Duxhurst Farm Colony for Inebriate Women in Kent. In 1913, readers of the *London Evening News* voted her 'the woman they would most like to be Britain's first female prime minister'.

During the First World War the Temperance movement achieved some success when the hours pubs were open were limited – restrictions that remained in place for over seventy years.

LADY SOMERSET. (LIBRARY OF CONGRESS, LC-USZ62-122280)

'BABY' SUFFRAGETTES
WERE AS YOUNG AS ELEVEN

SOME OF THE WOMEN WHO SUPPORTED THE CAUSE
were extremely young. One of the movement's youngest supporters was Dora Thewlis. Dora and her formidable mother Eliza were
founder members of the WSPU branch in Huddersfield, formed
in January 1907.

In March 1907, yet another bill failed in Parliament. Ten women
from the Huddersfield branch offered to join a march on
Westminster. Around 500 constables were waiting for the women
outside the Houses of Parliament. By 10 p.m. that night seventy-
five women had been arrested, seven of them from Huddersfield
– including Dora Thewlis. The main picture in the next day's newspapers was of Dora, called the 'Baby Suffragette' by the paper,
looking tiny and dishevelled, standing between two large policemen, her skirt undone from the fight. The magistrate imprisoned

ELIZABETH 'BESSIE' WATSON LEADING THE GREAT PAGEANT.
(LSE, 7JCC/O/02/022)

her for six days. He wrote to Dora's parents, saying that they had let Dora run 'great risks in coming to London unaccompanied'. He ended by saying that she would be returned home with 'her fare paid out of the poor-box'. Eliza wrote back saying that Dora had her own money, saved from her £1 a week earnings, and further that 'she was quite capable of taking care of herself'. She wrote to her daughter in prison to tell her about the letter from the judge, which finished by declaring that she was 'too young' and should have been in school. What ignorance, she pointed out: Dora, and girls much younger, were at the very moment working ten hours a day on a loom. Another 'baby Suffragette', Elizabeth 'Bessie' Watson, led the Great Pageant of 17 June 1911, at the age of eleven. Christabel Pankhurst herself later presented Bessie with a brooch depicting Queen Boudicca; Bessie sent it to Margaret Thatcher when she was elected Britain's first woman prime minister in 1979.

By way of comparison, Mrs Brackenbury was reputedly the oldest Suffragette prisoner, at seventy-eight. Older prisoners received no concessions: three grandmothers were imprisoned together in 1912, one of whom fell on the ice in an exercise yard. She broke several bones, but received no treatment until her release.

SUFFRAGETTES WERE LEADERS IN THE ANIMAL-RIGHTS MOVEMENT

MANY FEMINISTS AND SUFFRAGETTES WERE ALSO vegetarians and anti-vivisection campaigners, identifying with animals who, like women, were victims. In 1908, Maud Joachim claimed that the ranks of militant Suffragettes were mostly recruited from vegetarians. Frances Power Cobbe, executive council member of the NUWSS, founded the National Anti-Vivisection Society in 1875.

In 1902, Louise Lind and Liesa Schartau posed as students to observe experiments at London University. Their subsequent book *The Shambles of Science* described the cruel treatment of dogs there, leading to both a libel action and the erection of a now-famous statue in Battersea in September 1906: the Brown Dog. The inscription reads:

THE STATUE AT UNIVERSITY COLLEGE LONDON. (WELLCOME LIBRARY, LONDON)

> In Memory of the Brown Terrier Dog Done to Death in the Laboratories of University College in February 1903 after having endured Vivisections extending over more than two months and having been handed over from one Vivisector to another till Death came to his release. Also in memory of the 232 dogs vivisected in the same place during the year 1902. Men and Women of England: How long shall these things be?

The Suffragette Charlotte Despard spoke at the unveiling of the statue. Medical students attacked it the following year. Initially the local council provided a guard, but a new Conservative council removed the statue in 1909 – but not before Suffragettes and Trade Unionists had clashed with protesting medical students.

SUFFRAGETTES HAD THEIR OWN BOARD GAMES

THE SUFFRAGETTES WERE CONSUMMATE PUBLICISTS. When they organised an event, it had to be an impressive and photogenic spectacle.

They set up The Woman's Press in 1908, bringing together the production and distribution of all manner of propaganda. Some of the more popular items included Suffragette playing cards and a board game known as 'Pank-a-Squith', first advertised in *Votes for Women* on 22 October 1909. This popular game came with six painted lead figures. The board is stamped 'Made in Germany' on the back. The objective of each player was to get their Suffragette figure from their home to the Houses of Parliament, the pinnacle of achievement for the campaign for women's suffrage. Along the way they encountered obstacles such as police brutality, prison and force-feeding, which the player had to try their best to avoid.

Although designed to be humorous, the game none-theless revealed the dark reality of the campaign for suffrage.

'SUFFRAGETTES IN AND OUT OF PRISON'. (LSE, TWL/2004/1089)

THE MAGAZINE *VOTES FOR WOMEN* WAS SOLD IN WHSMITH

THE PUBLICATION *VOTES FOR WOMEN* WAS FOUNDED
with financial support from Emmeline and Frederick Pethick-
Lawrence, and vowed to offer 'a correct account of the doings of
the militant suffragists'.

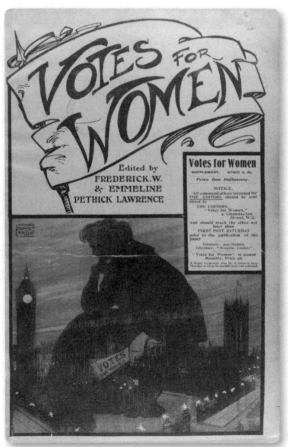

(LSE, N39)

Rather than produce a political tract, the paper aped the style of the popular press and was eminently readable. The magazine was heavily marketed and women who could not – or would not – involve themselves in acts of violence or civil disobedience instead supported the movement by spending many hours selling magazines on street corners. Edith Craig recalled:

> I love it. But I'm always getting moved on. You see, I generally sell the paper outside the Eustace Miles Restaurant, and I offer it verbally to every soul that passes. If they refuse, I say something to them. Most of them reply, others come up, and we collect a little crowd until I'm told to let the people into the restaurant, and move on. Then I begin all over again.

The magazine was a spearhead of WSPU campaigns, with sales of 16,000 copies in 1909, rising to 40,000 the following year; the total readership was estimated at upwards of 100,000 people. Eventually it became a weekly publication, sold for a penny. Printed in the Suffragette colours of purple, white and green, the magazine aimed to emphasise the heroic aspects of the campaign. Sylvia Pankhurst considered it to be 'the most effective propaganda organ' ever created: it was even sold in WHSmith. However, *Votes for Women* was not the only suffrage magazine. *The Freewoman*, founded by Dora Marsden after she left the WSPU and joined the WFL and produced between 1911 and 1912, promoted radical ideas around sexuality: it advocated free love and interpreted feminism more widely and radically than either the WSPU or the NUWSS. Millicent Fawcett, who tried to avoid any hint of sexual scandal being attached to the movement, described it as 'objectionable and mischievous, and tore it up into small pieces'.

MANY SUFFRAGETTES WERE CONCERNED ABOUT THEIR APPEARANCE

MANY SUFFRAGE CAMPAIGNERS CONFORMED TO Victorian and Edwardian ideals of ladylike demeanor. They campaigned by holding political teas, 'parasol parades' and bazaars, which they attended wearing gloves and large hats. Decked out in Suffragette colours of purple, white and green, supporters attempted to appear feminine and fashionable, which helped to undermine the vicious stereotypes of dowdy feminists then, as now, in circulation. As just one example, one Dr J.R. Benson gave a talk to the Bath Literary and Philosophical Society in which he described the 'Suffragette type' as 'excessively masculine'. This, he felt, would lead the 'nation to rot', and eventually to the extinction of mankind! His greatest disdain was for male supporters of the women's suffrage cause, whom he considered 'excessively feminine', men who were 'vain, wore pretty socks and ties and was only a sportsman to the extent of risking a few pence at a football match, where he was ever a looker on and never a participant … He was of little real use and if he married at all it was generally to one of his stronger-minded female friends… He was really a male anatomically, a female mentally, and nothing much physiologically.'

Suffragette clothing was branded. Department stores created items, including underwear and jewelry, in Suffragette colours, capitalising on wealthy ladies' desire to indicate their support for the movement: Jaeger introduced corsets 'especially for comfort in marching'. The London jeweller Mappen & Webb even produced a catalogue of Suffragette jewellery for Christmas in 1908. However, not all women could match this ideal: Hannah Mitchell, a working-class Suffragette who only possessed one old brown 'costume' (which she wore on every occasion), said she often felt shabby and out-of-place amongst her wealthier peers.

SUFFRAGETTES ONCE WHITEWASHED A HORSE FOR A PAGEANT

SUFFRAGE SOCIETIES WERE AWARE OF HOW PUBLICITY could be gained by spectacle and pageantry, and none used this more effectively than the WSPU. This extract, from *Memories of a Militant* by Annie Kenney, illustrates the importance placed on creating the perfect image.

(LSE)

During one of the big processions the idea was to have a white horse for a special feature. The day of the great event arrived. Only those behind the scenes saw the anxious looks on the faces … The news was whispered to me: the white horse had not appeared, and we were to start in fifteen minutes … What was to be done? Miss Dunlop rushed off to our friend and asked the reason for the appearance of a brown horse instead of a white one. Profuse apologies from our friend, and a promise that a white horse would be round in a minute. Five minutes passed. Another taxi was hailed. Miss Dunlop, very angry at the mistake, rushed into the stables and there was the brown horse practically finished. He was being whitewashed!

SUFFRAGETTES PUT PADDING UNDER THEIR CLOTHES TO PROTECT THEMSELVES FROM POLICE BRUTALITY

WHEN THE POLICE BROKE UP WOMEN'S SUFFRAGE demonstrations, their treatment of activists was less than gentle. When they attempted to reach Parliament and petition MPs, the women were often violently turned away by police.

On one occasion, rather than stage a large march on Parliament, it was decided that pairs of Suffragettes should set off from diverse parts of London to converge on Westminster. Alice Paul, an American women's rights campaigner who spent some time in Britain and took an active role in suffrage activities, startled her partner when she arrived at their six o'clock rendezvous: she had suddenly gained a great deal of weight, and in fact was near-unrecognisable. Her partner pointed this out. 'We are going to be in the hands of your police presently,' she replied, 'and I am told they are rough about it so I've padded myself.' When she was indeed manhandled by the police, the strained buttons on her clothes began to pop – whereupon the 'entrails of some woolly monster emerged roll upon roll'. The surprised onlookers shouted, 'oh, look at the stuffing!' and she was cheered as the police carted Alice and her coils of wool away.

Alice was arrested several times during her years as a Suffragette, and served three prison sentences before returning to the USA.

ALICE PAUL (LSE, LC-DIG-HEC-12352) AND WITH MRS PETHICK-LAWRENCE. (LSE LC-USZ62-126547)

SUFFRAGETTE VEHICLES INCLUDED A PROTEST CARAVAN

MURIEL MATTERS USED A HORSE-DRAWN CARAVAN to get her message into inaccessible rural areas of the country, where the cause of women's suffrage was almost unknown.

She and a team of intrepid travellers, with their horse (named Asquith, after the prime minister) and a caravan brightly painted in suffrage colours, travelled all over southern England. They were received enthusiastically in some places but faced apple cores, rotten fruit and 'hostile roughs' intent on preventing them from speaking in others. Margaret Newinson recalled later the very antagonistic reception at Herne Bay, where their caravan was pushed along the seafront to cries of 'Chuck 'em in the sea!' Thankfully, a group of fisherman helped them and stood guard 'while outside the mob howled like wild beasts till a late hour'.

Muriel conducted many other publicity stunts, including chaining herself to the grille in the Ladies Gallery of the Houses of Parliament (popping the padlock key down the front of her dress with a cry of 'votes for women!'). She later dropped 56lb of leaflets across London from the basket of an airship, and chartered a boat to sail past the terrace of the Houses of Parliament, from which she hailed the tea-drinking MPs through a loud-speaker.

(LSE, TWL.2002.621)

MEN OF BRIXTON DEMAND

THE FIRST FEMALE CHAUFFEUR IN BRITAIN WAS A SUFFRAGETTE

IN 1909, IT WAS DECIDED THAT EMMELINE PANKHURST and Emmeline Pethick-Lawrence should have the use of a car, so a new Austin motor-car was purchased in the Suffragette colours of purple, white and green. Vera 'Jack' Holme was chosen to be their driver, even though Mrs Pankhurst had doubts about her ability. As Vera later confessed, 'Mrs Pankhurst thought I was very giddy and she wasn't at all for having me because I used to act the galoot in the office.' Vera seems to have overcome Mrs Pankhurst's qualms after driving her around Scotland without misfortune. Vera was by no means conventional: she smoked, dressed in men's clothes whenever she could and had supported herself by working as a music-hall singer and male impersonator to supplement a small allowance from her father. She liked to be known by her nickname, 'Jack', and had romantic liaisons with women. Her driving prowess was praised in 1911, when she was named as the first woman chauffeur in Britain by *The Chauffeur* magazine.

VERA 'JACK' HOLME. (LSE. 7VJH/5/2/03)

One of Vera's greatest adventures came when she and another Suffragette, Elsie Howey, disrupted a Liberal Party election rally in Bristol in May 1909. Women were banned from the meeting in Colston Hall. As a protest, WSPU members rented a house opposite and used a megaphone to disrupt the proceeding from there. Elsie and Vera's more daring plan involved sneaking into the Hall during the afternoon and climbing onto a narrow platform behind the organ pipes, where they waited for three hours. Despite a police search, they were not discovered – and shouted 'Votes for Women' through the organ pipes as soon as the Liberal MP, Augustine Birrell, began to speak. It took ten minutes for the police to discover their hiding place. Vera and Elsie's voices being magnified through the organ pipes, and the women in the house opposite using their megaphones – it must have created quite a cacophony. Vera later wrote a parody of the famous Victorian song 'The Lost Chord':

> Seated one day in the organ
> We were weary and ill at ease;
> We sat there three hours only,
> Hid, midst the dusty keys …

THE WSPU HAD THEIR OWN CHAIN OF SHOPS

THE MOVEMENT RAISED FUNDS BY THE SALE OF JAMS, marmalades and all manner of 'fancy goods', either made or donated by members and initially sold at bazaars. For example, the Women's Freedom League held a 'Green, White and Gold Fancy Fair' at Caxton Hall; Suffragette sewing parties were held beforehand to prepare items for display. The WSPU women's exhibition at the Prince's Skating Ring in 1909 awarded a prize for the best Suffragette blouse 'suitable for practical wear'. The success of these events was matched by WSPU stores set up across the country including, from 1910, a department store on Charing Cross Road, close to Oxford Street.

All sorts of products (postcards, bags, belts, badges, hatpins, sashes, china, matches, playing cards – even underwear) were sold in the suffrage colours, including 'Votes for Women' brand tea (with matching caddies). One lady apparently bought 60lb of the tea in the first week of the store's opening. The shops also served as meeting places, both before and after demonstrations and rallies; they were somewhere where tactics could be discussed and protest banners stored. Several shops also held meetings and 'At Homes' in the evenings, attracting new members to the cause. For example, in 1909 the Lewisham shop recruited fifteen new members in the first week of opening. As militancy escalated, Suffragette shops were ransacked, and their windows were smashed in retaliation for the damage to property inflicted by Suffragettes on others.

'JUSTICE TEA.' (LSE, 7EWD/F/5/1)

030 SOME SUFFRAGETTES WERE GRAFFITI ARTISTS

ON 22 JUNE 1909 MARION WALLACE DUNLOP, a sculptress, attempted to print an extract from the Bill of Rights on the wall of St Stephen's Hall in the House of Commons. Ejected without being arrested, she returned two days later and stamped the quotation on the wall with indelible ink. This time she was taken into custody. Many Suffragettes spent their days chalking 'votes for women' onto pavements, while others concentrated on fly-posting all the churches, letter boxes and public buildings in a particular area at night.

Even these peaceful activities could end in a prison sentence, as magistrates imposed heavy penalties on repeat offenders. Catherine Margesson and Nurse Evans, two such Suffragettes, were both fined £1 and given seven days in prison for obstructing the footway in the Strand after they chalked 'votes for women' onto the pavement in 1909. Their individual fines, equivalent to a week's wages for many, were paid for them by generous supporters of the cause. Other means of using graffiti to raise awareness included the defacement of coins; mutilating them was an ideal medium for spreading the message, as the pennies would then circulate widely through all sections of society, and were rarely recalled by the Bank despite the political message they now carried.

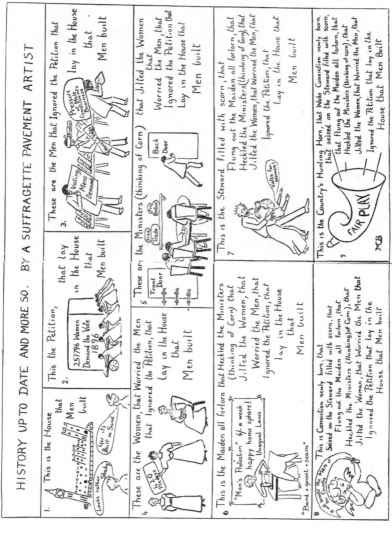

'SUFFRAGE PAVEMENT ARTISTS.' (LSE, 10/54)

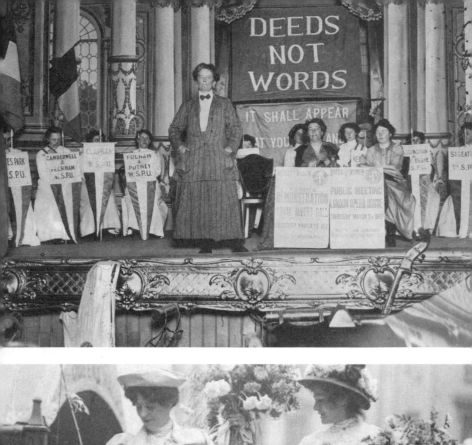

EMMELINE PANKHURST IS RUMOURED TO HAVE HAD LESBIAN AFFAIRS

CONTROVERSY AND DEBATE STILL SURROUNDS whether leading Suffragettes including Christabel Pankhurst, Annie Kenney, Emily Wilding Davison and Mary Leigh were lesbians – and, if so, the degree to which this may have been shaped by their suffrage activities or influenced the movement as a whole.

One of Emmeline's rumoured lovers was Suffragette composer Dame Ethel Smyth, who wrote the March of Women anthem for the Coronation Procession in 1911. The anthem was dedicated to Emmeline. Suffragette prisoners sung Ethel's anthem to keep their spirits up in prison. When Ethel herself was incarcerated, she conducted other prisoners through the window of her cell with a toothbrush. Other inspirational anthems, such as Shoulder to Shoulder and Rise Up Women, were sung on marches, at meetings and demonstrations and by prisoners. The Women's Marseillaise (written by Florence Macaulay, a school teacher who became a WSPU organiser) demanded that women should be free, whilst March of the Women, by Cicely Hamilton, declared: 'Cry with the wind for the dawn is breaking! March, march, swing you along, Wide blows our banner and hope is waking.' However, Suffragettes didn't have it all their own way: music-hall songs often made fun of the Suffragettes, as in this popular song:

Put me on an island where the girls are few,
Put me amongst the most ferocious lions in the zoo,
Put me on a treadmill, and I'll never fret
But for pity's sake don't put me with a Suffragette!

ETHEL SMYTH (LSE, 7JCC/O/02/005) AND MARY LEIGH (LSE, 7JCC/O/02/044A), BOTH OF WHOM WERE RUMOURED TO HAVE HAD AFFAIRS WITH OTHER SUFFRAGETTES.

THE FIRST WOMAN TO MARRY WITHOUT PROMISING TO OBEY WAS A SUFFRAGETTE

UNA DUGDALE WAS A SUPPORTER OF THE WSPU. In 1909 she organised a Women's Suffrage Ball to raise funds, and later that same year was imprisoned after a demonstration in Parliament Square.

Then, in January 1912, she married Victor Duval at the Savoy Chapel, where she caused controversy by abandoning the traditional approach to the marriage ceremony: her father did not 'give her away', and she was also the first woman to remove the commitment to obey her husband from the marriage vows. A pamphlet written by her, entitled 'Love and Honour – but not Obey', was published in 1912. Una was not the only Suffragette to challenge normal expectations for Edwardian matrimony: Teresa Billington, who also had the honour of being the first Suffragette to be sent to Holloway Prison, met and married Glasgow businessman and socialist Frederick Lewis Greig; the pair met during her time as an organiser for the WSPU. They agreed to adopt a new name as a pair, both being known as Billington-Greig from that day on.

NAPKIN COMMEMORATING THE MARRIAGE OF MR HUGH A. FRANKLIN AND MISS ELSIE D. DUVAL, SISTER OF VICTOR DUVAL, AND BOTH FELLOW SUFFRAGISTS. (LSE, 7HFD/D/01)

SOME MPS CLAIMED WOMEN DID NOT WANT THE VOTE

IN 1908, A WOMEN'S SUFFRAGE BILL PASSED ITS second reading in Parliament with a majority of 179. It proposed that women should be allowed to vote on the same limited terms as men, namely that they must be householders or married to householders (thereby withholding the vote from most of the working class).

A heated debate followed. Charles Mallett, Plymouth's Liberal MP, opposed the bill, disparaging the countries which had already given the vote to women. Australia and New Zealand were 'young colonies with limited political experience and their rather crude political methods', he declared. The four American states that had enfranchised women also came in for criticism: Idaho and Wyoming consisted of 'mining camps and cattle ranches'; Colorado was 'one of the worse governed states of the union'; and Utah was simply dismissed as 'the Mormon State'. Nationalist MP Sir Walter Nugent, meanwhile, argued that most women did not want the vote – so why force it on them? He asked, 'Was it because a small and noisy minority were making the days and nights of Cabinet ministers hideous with their howlings?' He ended by saying that since women had been given the County Council franchise, he had never met a woman who did not look upon it as a nuisance.

Philip Snowden, meanwhile, who was in favour of the bill, spoilt his defence rather by ending his speech by declaring that, in countries that had given women the vote, 'the stockings still got darned, the baby was still nursed'.

LORD PHILIP SNOWDEN. (LSE, TWL.2000.90)

SUFFRAGETTES USED ACID IN THEIR ATTACKS

IN THE 1909 ELECTION IN BERMONDSEY, SUFFRAGETTES poured acid into ballot boxes, causing minor injury to the election officer (an event which the *Pall Mall Gazette* described, rather untruthfully, as 'an outrage unparalleled in English history'). The two WFL (Women's Freedom League) members involved, Alison Neilans and Alice Chapin, were each given the draconian sentence of seven months' imprisonment.

A similar incident in Battersea caused Mr Elias Marshall to suffer slight burns to his hands and right eye when a Suffragette attempted to destroy leaflets and canvassing cards by throwing acid over them. She then escaped on a bicycle. Post Office workers also burnt their hands emptying postal pillar boxes in which Suffragettes had placed acid. The postal service was an important mode of communication at the time, and pouring ink, lampblack or tar into postal pillar boxes was an effective method of destruction; the boxes were sometimes set on fire afterwards, just to be truly thorough. In December 1912, Suffragettes tipped paint and ink into a postbox in Windsor, rendering approximately 1,000 Christmas cards and letters indecipherable. The loss caused great inconvenience, and garnered public censure as a result. Attacks by suffrage campaigners against ordinary citizens' personal property marked a new phase in the campaigns. The *New York Times* wrote scathingly: 'there is something of a sacredness of posted letters that even savages recognise.' The paper also noted that, though men had previously performed similar 'outrageous acts' in pursuit of their rights, such acts often 'marred the progress of good causes towards success', and counselled women against repeating the 'vicious stupidity of their brothers'.

MEN STOOD FOR PARLIAMENT AS SUFFRAGE CANDIDATES

035

THE ARISTOCRATIC PHILOSOPHER AND MATHEMATICIAN Bertrand Russell stood on a women's suffrage ticket in Wimbledon. Two thousand people attended the meeting that opened his campaign – which quickly descended into chaos after opponents released rats into the hall to frighten the women in attendance. Following a lively campaign, during which eggs were thrown and many of the meetings were disturbed, Henry Chaplin, a Conservative who opposed women's suffrage, achieved a record majority of 6,964.

Another man who stood as a suffrage candidate was George Lansbury, the MP for Bow and Bromley (and also grandfather of the much-loved actress Angela Lansbury). His support for the cause was well known, and led him into some interesting moments, including the time he was ordered to leave the House of Commons for shaking his fist at Prime Minister Asquith, telling him he was 'beneath contempt' for his treatment of Suffragette prisoners. He resigned his seat to force a by-election in October 1912, which he then fought on a 'votes for women' platform. However, Lansbury's campaign was not helped by the WSPU leadership's rather half-hearted support: despite his personal popularity, he was to find that many working-class men of the East End were violently opposed to the concept of equal rights for women. He lost the election by 731 votes.

GEORGE LANSBURY. (LSE, 7JCC O 0114I)

ONE SUFFRAGETTE LEADER STARTED HER CAREER AS A ROMANTIC NOVELIST

MRS PANKHURST WAS NOT THE ONLY RADICAL LEADER. The Women's Freedom League (WFL), which was formed in 1907, elected Charlotte Despard as its president in 1909. Charlotte Despard had a long and varied career in public life. Following her marriage in 1870, Charlotte had pursued a career as a novelist, writing ten novels, mainly romantic love stories with titles which included *Chaste as Ice, Pure as Snow* (1874) and *The Rajah's Heir: A Novel* (1890). She was committed to peace, tax resistance and working with the Labour Party, and was popular with her membership.

Despard's interests were diverse, and her black clothing and sandals distinctive. Initially a Roman Catholic, she took up Theosophy in 1899. She was a Poor Law Guardian in Lambeth, London, in 1894, and an unsuccessful Labour candidate for Parliament in 1918; a vegetarian, she became vice president of the London Vegetarian Society in 1931. She was a supporter of Sinn Féin – even though her brother, John French, was Lord Lieutenant of Ireland in 1921 – and she died in Ireland in 1939.

SUFFRAGETTE PROPERTY SEIZED BY THE POLICE INCLUDED ROYAL DIAMONDS

SOPHIA DULEEP SINGH WAS THE DAUGHTER OF Maharajah Duleep Singh. A goddaughter of Queen Victoria, she lived a life of wealth and privilege, taking her place in the highest rungs of fashionable society. She lived in rooms at Hampton Court Palace. However, the princess was also passionately political: her campaigns against injustice included fighting for Indian independence and for women's suffrage. Her membership of the WSPU was a publicity coup for the organisation, and was astutely used as a means of raising funds: her jams, for example, were an extremely popular addition to many suffrage bazaars. Her celebrity status meant she took a prominent position in demonstrations or meetings.

Sophia's militancy took many forms, including refusing to pay for such dues as her dog licences; she also refused to pay the charges owing for keeping servants and her carriage tax. When her case went to court, however, the judge was reluctant to give the WSPU the publicity that imprisoning an Indian princess would provide. The bailiffs were therefore instructed to enter her property and recover goods to the amount of the fines due. They chose her seven-stone diamond ring. It was auctioned and immediately purchased by another Suffragette – Louise Jopling Rowe – who returned it to Sophia as the other women applauded.

A number of other Indian women in the UK offered their support to the suffrage movement, participating in marches, selling newspapers and otherwise working to raise funds for the cause.

(LSE, TWL 2002 638)

Women's Tax Resistance League.

TELEPHONE: 3385 CITY.
10, TALBOT HOUSE,
98, ST. MARTIN'S LANE,
W.C.

No Taxation Without Representation.

The Princess Sophia Duleep Singh's Goods will be sold for Tax Resistance, on Tues. July 25th at Hicks, Station Rd. Ashford. Meeting to be held in Auction Rooms after Sale

Please come and bring friends to support Protest

Meeting at 4 o'clock.
Waterloo 2.10. to Ashford 2/6 return.

GANDHI SUPPORTED VOTES FOR WOMEN

IN 1909 THE WLF LEADER, CHARLOTTE DESPARD, met Mohandas Karamchand Gandhi, then a young lawyer in London, through her involvement in the Vegetarian Society.

They discussed the WFL's commitment to civil disobedience rather than any form of violence. Gandhi supported the suffrage movement, whilst making it clear he did not approve of the more militant activities of stone-throwing, brawling with the police and attacks on private property. The WFL also disapproved of violent means of protest, although they did support the use of what they considered 'vigorous agitation'. In 1908 and 1909, League members chained themselves to various objects in Parliament in order to protest against the government. On 28 October 1908, for example, three members of the Women's Freedom League, Muriel Matters, Violet Tillard, and Helen Fox, released a banner at the House of Commons. The women also chained themselves to the grille above a window. Law enforcement had to remove the grille while they were still attached to it before they could file off the locks that held them connected to the window. This protest became known as the Grille Incident.

Other protests by the League included the then-radical suggestion, by one of their members, that the WLF should help working women to gain access to contraception, allowing them to limit the size of their families until such a time as all women won the vote. However, many League members disapproved of this idea. The League's members opposed the First World War, and in 1914 their conference discussed crippling the Bank of England by finding ways to deplete its gold reserves. More popular measures they did successfully carry out included bill-posting campaigns, deputations to Parliament and padlocking themselves to court buildings. The League also protested by refusing to complete the 1911 census forms and by not paying taxes.

GANDHI WITH EMMELINE PETHICK-LAWRENCE'S HUSBAND FREDERICK.
(LSE, 7JCC/O/02/135)

SUFFRAGETTES MADE MASS RUNS ON PARLIAMENT

SUFFRAGETTES STRUGGLED TO GET PARLIAMENT TO listen to their arguments. Knowing that no meetings or demonstrations were allowed within a mile of the Houses of Parliament, they came up with an audacious plan. Twenty to thirty Suffragettes hid inside a furniture van; on arrival at the House of Commons, the women leapt out and attempted to gain entrance. Unfortunately the police had been tipped off, but their daring attempt on Parliament nonetheless gained the cause a great deal of publicity. The newspapers christened it 'The Trojan Horse' affair, and the story went global: papers as far afield as the *Chicago Herald Tribune* reported the story.

On another occasion, an attempt was made to gain entrance to the House of Lords: six large vans drove up to the House, and ten to twelve well-dressed Suffragettes sprang out as the doors opened. They proceeded to hold a meeting until they were dragged away – again causing much interest and merriment in the next day's newspapers.

CHRISTABEL PANKHURST, FLORA DRUMMOND AND EMMELINE PANKHURST IN COURT, 1908; THEY WERE CHARGED WITH SEDITION AFTER ORGANISING 'RUSHES' OF PARLIAMENT. (LSE, 7JCC/O/02/060 AND LSE, 7JCC/O/02/061)

EMILY WILDING DAVISON WAS NOT THE FIRST WOMAN TO DIE FOR THE CAUSE

EMMELINE PANKHURST WAS NOT THE ONLY Suffragette in her family. Mary Jane Clarke, her sister, helped her to found the WSPU, and also worked tirelessly to promote the cause. She was to contribute more than almost any other woman, becoming the first woman to die as a result of her suffrage activities.

She had been imprisoned twice, and been a paid organiser of the WSPU in Brighton. She took part in the Black Friday march on the House of Commons in November 1910, where she was involved in scuffles with the police and numbered among the 156 women arrested and sent to Holloway Prison. By the time she was released she was in a severely weakened state. On 23 December she spoke at a WSPU 'welcome' luncheon, but two days later, on Christmas Day, she collapsed. She died after suffering a brain haemorrhage, attributed to the cruel treatment she had received whilst in police custody and the strain of her prison sentence. She was just forty-eight years old. Mary Clarke was quietly buried. Her death was not given much publicity, as a General Election had been called for January 1911 and the WSPU hoped that they would achieve their aims in the next Parliament. Sadly, as we now know, that was not to be.

A very different funeral was to follow upon the death of the cause's most famous martyr, Emily Wilding Davison. Emily died from injuries sustained when she ran onto the racecourse during the Derby in the summer of 1913 and was struck by Anmer, the King's own horse. Her funeral, meticulously planned and carried out, caused a national sensation.

EMILY WILDING DAVISON FALLS. (LSE, TWL/2004/321)

SUFFRAGETTES STAGED SEX-STRIKE COMEDIES AND OTHER FEMINIST THEATRE

NUMEROUS ACTRESSES, THEATRE MANAGERS AND writers actively promoted women's suffrage, putting on propaganda plays and pageants or joining and supporting the Actresses Franchise League (AFL). The AFL often worked with the Women Writers' Suffrage League (WWSL).

In 1909 Cicely Hamilton wrote *A Pageant of Great Women*, a massive spectacle in which Suffragettes dressed up as famous historical women. Edith Craig, who later worked at the Little Theatre in London, directed it. The following year, in 1910, the opening play at the Little Theatre was *Lysistrata*, with Gertrude Kingston, the actor and manager of the theatre, in the title role. Laurence Houseman had translated and paraphrased the Ancient Greek comic play, in which women seek to get their husbands to end the Peloponnesian War by withholding sex. His version of the play was then published by the Women's Press.

Edith Craig and her partner Christopher St John also founded their own women's theatre company, based in London. 'Christopher' was actually Christabel Marshall, an extraordinary woman who worked as a secretary for Lady Randolph Churchill (and for her son Winston on occasions too). She lived with Edith and another woman, artist Clare 'Tony' Atwood, in a ménage-à-trois for more than thirty years. Their company, known as the Pioneer Players, put on single performances of plays that would never be produced in the commercial theatre. The plays were feminist and used women as actresses, writers, directors, designers, and also in traditional male jobs such as accounting and lighting. The Players ran from 1911 to 1914, attracting a mainly female audience.

EDITH CRAIG. (LSE, TWL 2009 02 61)

Votes for women.
Edith Craig[?]

NOT ALL SUFFRAGETTES WERE ABLE-BODIED

DISABILITY WAS NO BAR TO CAMPAIGNING. ROSA MAY Billinghurst, who joined the WSPU in 1907, was unable to walk without crutches. She used a special tricycle wheelchair to get around, often decked out in the WSPU colours of purple, white and green.

May often took an active part in demonstrations. Too active for the establishment's liking, as it turned out: as she later told the suffrage press, the police 'took me down a side road and left me in the middle of a hooligan crowd, first taking all the valves out of the wheels and pocketing them so I could not move the machine'. Undeterred, her antics became infamous within suffrage circles. May fought endlessly with the police, sometimes charging them in her chair (which she also used to hide bricks to throw through windows or chemicals to put into postboxes). On one occasion she was arrested and, still in her tricycle, carried shoulder high by four policemen whilst the crowds cheered her.

Sadly, May's more active contributions to the struggle came to an abrupt end. She was forcibly fed in prison in 1913, suffering the invasive procedure for ten days, three times a day, despite being very frail on top of her disability. The tube the prison doctors forced through her nose and down her throat into her stomach caused 'almost incredible suffering', and when she was released she was 'a physical wreck'.

TWO SUFFRAGETTES, IN THIS CASE MARY LEIGH AND EDITH NEW, BEING RELEASED FROM HOLLOWAY PRISON. (LSE, 7JCC/O/02/040)

ROSA MAY BILLINGHURST. (LSE, TWL 2002 22)

SUFFRAGETTES BOYCOTTED THE 1911 CENSUS

RALLYING BEHIND THE SLOGAN 'IF WOMEN DO NOT count, neither shall they be counted', some Suffragettes boycotted the 1911 census. They could not be included if not at home, and so women hid in all sorts of places to avoid being counted: the roller-skating rink at the Aldwych, where the skating continued for nine and a half very cold hours; a vegetarian restaurant; and famously, of course, in a House of Commons' cupboard. However, newspapers trivialised the protest by suggesting that the real reason that women did not wish to be included was that they did not want to disclose their age! The satirical magazine *Punch* had perhaps the cleverest response, quipping that 'women had lost their census'.

One interesting census form unearthed by Jill Liddington is that of Eleanora Maund of West Kensington. Eleanora's name is crossed through on the schedule. However, her husband must have intercepted it, as he has added the following note, in red pen: 'My wife unfortunately being a Suffragette put her pen through her name, but it must stand as correct. It being an equivocation to say she is away. She being always resident here and has only attempted by a silly subterfuge to defeat the object of the census to which as "Head" of the family I object.' The letter was signed E. A. Maund.

DECIMA MOORE, AN ACTRESS AND ONE OF MANY SUFFRAGETTES TO DODGE THE 1911 CENSUS BY ATTENDING THE ALDWYCH SKATING RINK. (LSE, 7JCC/O/02/139)

THE WSPU WERE BANNED FROM THE ROYAL ALBERT HALL

SOME OF THE BIGGEST GATHERINGS OF WOMEN ever held in Britain were organised by Suffragettes.

One rally in 1908, attended by 300,000 people, included no less than 70 bands, 20 platforms, 80 women speakers and 700 banners. Special trains enabled supporters from all over the country to attend; luncheon was served, at 2 shillings (or tea, cake and bread and butter at ninepence), to ensure that no one arrived hungry. From Bradford the fare was 11 shillings – prohibitively expensive

A LEAFLET FOR A ROYAL ALBERT HALL RALLY. (LSE. 2ASL/11/01A-C)

for many working-class women. Nevertheless, women travelled from Northern England, Wales and Scotland. Sixty came from Huddersfield alone, seven of whom were later arrested.

Suffragettes held some of their biggest indoor rallies at the Royal Albert Hall. Then, in October 1912, Emmeline addressed her supporters from its stage, declaring: 'I incite this meeting to rebellion! Be militant each in your own way; I accept full responsibility for everything you do.' Over the next few months, as a result, the Trustees of the Hall came under pressure to ban the WSPU. One letter, sent on 21 March by a Mr P.S. Bridgeford and addressed to the Earl of Kilmorey, encapsulates some of the public's feeling on the matter. 'My Lord,' he writes, 'may I beg to suggest whether the time has now arrived when the directors of the Royal Albert Hall should reconsider their attitude in letting their Hall to an organisation which is carrying on a criminal campaign involving the destruction of public and private property.'

A few weeks later, in April 1913, the Trustees of the Hall banned Emmeline Pankhurst, her daughters and the WSPU from further use of the Hall. The ban was not lifted until March 1918 – when a Patriotic Meeting and Celebration of the Women's Suffrage Victory was held there!

MANY SUFFRAGETTES WERE KEEN CYCLISTS

THE AMERICAN SUFFRAGETTE SUSAN B. ANTHONY suggested the bicycle had 'done more to emancipate women than anything else in the world. It gives women a feeling of freedom and self-reliance.'

The Elswick bicycle for ladies was specially produced, with enamelling in WSPU colours, to appeal to supporters of women's suffrage who enjoyed the freedom cycling offered. One group of Suffragette cyclists used this freedom rather boldly, flinging themselves en masse in front of Winston Churchill's motor-car in what was seen as a 'fresh development of militant tactics'. The women then used the mobility provided by their bicycles to effect their escape.

SUFFRAGETTES HAD THEIR OWN MEDALS

SUFFRAGETTE PRISONERS WERE OFTEN HAILED AS celebrities upon their release from incarceration. Their supporters were often waiting for them at the prison gates. Sometimes they were given celebratory breakfast or dinners, such as the complimentary banquet held for released prisoners at the Savoy Hotel on 11 December 1906: Mrs Fawcett of the NUWSS held the chair, whilst music was provided by the Aeolian Ladies Orchestra. Suffragette celebrities such as Emmeline Pankhurst were often released at unexpected or early hours of the day in an attempt to avoid the publicity surrounding these receptions.

Prisoners were also awarded badges or medals to commemorate their bravery. The Holloway Brooch, designed by Sylvia Pankhurst, was awarded to some members of the WSPU. Regarded as the Victoria Cross of the Union, the badge was fashioned in the shape of a silver portcullis in imitation of the symbol of the House of Commons. Superimposed over this was the broad arrow of conflict, enamelled in the purple, white and green colours of the movement. Holloway Brooch holders included Mary Eleanor Gawthorpe, a resilient member from a poor, working-class background who had achieved a double first from Leeds University. She was released from Holloway in 1908 but was imprisoned again in 1912 for breaking a window at the Home Office. Having served time with campaigners such as Dora Montefiore, Mary bravely embarked on a hunger and thirst strike. She was released after thirty-six hours.

Other awards included ribbons of a military style to which additional bars were awarded to indicate specific sufferings: a silver bar for hunger strike without force-feeding; a purple, white and green bar for hunger strike with force-feeding.

SUFFRAGETTE 'CRIMES' INCLUDED FAILING TO LICENSE A DEAD DOG

APPROXIMATELY 1,085 WOMEN AND 40 MALE SUFFRAGE activists were imprisoned, and many more appeared in court during the Suffragette campaigns. The length of sentences Suffragettes received now seem excessive in relation to their crimes: Emmeline was given three years for 'inciting violence'; six women were imprisoned for ringing the prime minister's doorbell; and Emily Wilding Davison was given a six-month sentence for setting fire to a pillar box.

In the spirit of 'no taxation without representation', activists refused to pay for everyday items such as dog licences. Emma Sproson, a working-class suffragist from Wolverhampton, was fined 2s 6d and costs for refusing to pay for a licence for her pet. She refused to pay the fine too. Her husband was charged with aiding and abetting; Emma had told him that if he paid the licence fee, 'I shall look upon you as a tyrant and not a husband.' When the court asked what Emma would have done if her husband had asked her either to get rid of the dog, pay the fee or leave the house, she told them she would've taken the last option – to loud laughter in the courtroom. On 23 May 1911, at Wolverhampton Court, she was sentenced to prison for seven days for non-payment of both her dog licence and the resulting fine – despite the dog in question having died the day before. Another woman, Miss Andrews of Ipswich, was similarly gaoled for one week for refusing to pay her dog licence.

CHARLOTTE DESPARD, EDITH HOW MARTIN AND EMMA SPROSON (WHO REFUSED TO PAY HER LICENCE FEE), IN 1914. (LSE, 7JCC/O/02/067)

SUFFRAGETTES RENTED THE HOUSE BEHIND HOLLOWAY PRISON

AS A WAY OF DEFYING THE AUTHORITIES, Suffragettes rented a house behind Holloway Prison – shouting encouragements across to inmates with the aid of a microphone. When in prison, acts of camaraderie such as these helped to keep up the prisoners' spirits. Supporters in the Holloway house also sang The March of the Women and the Marseillaise at full volume; this would have been fully audible to the prisoners, especially at night (when the women's spirits were often at their lowest). Vera Holme, Mrs Pankhurst's driver, was one of these singers. She had sung in the chorus of the D'Oyly Carte opera company, so she had a strong voice.

In the prison yard, women, including Emmeline Pankhurst, played games such as 'Here We Come Gathering Nuts in May' with gusto. They also played football, held a sports day, performed A Midsummer Night's Dream, and organised a fancy-dress contest, all inside the prison's walls. These acts helped to keep the women's resolve strong. They even managed to pass notes of solidarity to each other during Sunday services. As a final defiant touch, the prisoners added the message 'votes for women' into the shirts they were required to sew for their prison work.

EDITH NEW AND MARY LEIGH RUNNING OUT OF HOLLOWAY PRISON.
(LSE, 7EWD J 05)

SUFFRAGETTE PRISONERS HAD NO UNDERWEAR

NO KNICKERS, CORSETS OR EVEN SANITARY TOWELS were provided to the women serving time for suffrage-related sentences.

In August 1908, R.C. Wyatt, the husband of a suffrage supporter, wrote to Herbert Gladstone, the Home Secretary, about the failure of the prison authorities to provide Suffragette prisoners with sanitary towels. With typically Edwardian reticence, he attempted to make his complaint clear entirely using euphemisms, asking why, 'at certain times, certain indispensible clothing is not provided'. He asked the Home Secretary to stop this 'filthy punishment', which he viewed as 'an outrage on decency and health'.

We do not know if he ever received a reply, but there is certainly some evidence that having, for perhaps the first time, a set of female prisoners, many of them middle class and with excellent connections, who were vociferous in their complaints – both to the government and to the public – about the circumstances in which they were incarcerated eventually improved prison conditions.

EMMELINE AND CHRISTABEL PANKHURST IN MOCK PRISON GARB.
(LSE, 7JCC/O/02/070)

SOME HUSBANDS PAID SUFFRAGETTES' FINES SO THEY COULD COME HOME AND DO THE HOUSEWORK

A NUMBER OF SUFFRAGETTES WERE MARRIED. Many had children. It was often much harder for those with domestic responsibilities to contribute to the struggle. In an age with no expectation that the household work should be shared, the husbands of Suffragettes sometimes paid their fines simply so they could return to do the housework. Mrs Hannah Mitchell was one such woman.

Many husbands were likewise unsympathetic to the cause. Mrs Towler from the Preston branch of the WSPU was married to a supervisor in a textile factory and had four sons. Before she joined the Hyde Park rally in 1908, she had to ensure that her house was immaculate; she spent the entire previous week cooking and baking so the five men at home had enough food to keep them going for a fortnight (in case she was imprisoned). In 1912, meanwhile, middle-class Suffragette Eva Keller was locked in the larder all night by her husband to prevent her from going on a window-smashing raid. She sent her daughter Phyllis instead. The young woman was duly caught and imprisoned in Holloway.

A SUFFRAGETTE POSTER FROM 1909. (LSE, TWL.1999.15)

HOW THE LAW 'PROTECTS THE WIFE.'

WIFE: "Sir, can you help me, my husband earns 30/- a week and only gives me 5/- for food for myself and children."

LAW: "I cannot help you my good woman, your husband need only keep you alive, that is one of the laws of England."

THE PRISON FORCE-FEEDING TEAMS WERE LED BY DOCTORS

MANY DOCTORS WERE UNSYMPATHETIC TOWARDS the suffrage movement and Suffragette prisoners.

Doctors took an active role in forced feeding. It was a dangerous proposition to insert a tube down the throat of a struggling woman: risks included blocking the patient's airway by inserting the tube into the lungs rather than the stomach; potential complications included pleurisy or fatal pneumonia. The physical after-effects of the feeding were severe: bruising of the face, nose and throat; damage to teeth; nausea and vomiting; stomach cramps and diarrhoea. Lilian Lenton, a twenty-one-year-old who lived in Bristol but travelled all over the country carrying out law-breaking activities on behalf of the WSPU, was arrested in 1913, in Doncaster, charged with throwing stones. She was force-fed but quickly released after the process went tragically awry: the feeding tube slipped and speared into her lungs; then the doctors, not realising the tube was not settled in her stomach, poured gruel down it. She was lucky to survive, and only lived because she was young and fit. The prison, anxious to avoid her dying in prison, ordered her release.

Given the dangers involved in the process, it was surprising more doctors did not protest against the procedure. However, this may have had something to do with the fact that the president of the Royal College of Physicians, a fervent anti-suffragist, was a personal friend of Prime Minister Asquith. He may have silenced the profession's complaints, as there was little serious opposition until 1912. A study was then published in *The Lancet* detailing the case studies of ninety Suffragettes who had suffered damage to their cardiovascular, gastrointestinal and nervous systems because of the tortures the prison service subjected them to. It took another year or two, until 1913–1914, for enough doctors to group together to raise meaningful objections to the deployment of this barbaric 'treatment'.

THIS CONTEMPORARY CARTOON ABOUT SUFFRAGETTE HUNGER STRIKES RATHER UNDERPLAYS THE HORRIFIC AND LONG-LASTING EFFECTS OF THE 'TREATMENT' ON THE WOMEN WHO ENDURED IT. (LIBRARY OF CONGRESS, LC-USZC2-1063)

SUFFRAGETTE PRISONERS PRETENDED TO BE VEGETARIAN

A HUMANE WARDRESS IN HOLLOWAY TOLD HER regular clients to pretend they were vegetarians when re-arrested so they could get better rations. This information quickly spread. Vegetarian prisoners were given extra milk and butter, and an egg was added to their meagre prison rations (which was much preferred to the tough meat or broth alternatives). When hunger striking, Suffragettes also found that vegetarian liquid, force-fed, was easier on their bodies than a fatty meat or Bovril. When Suffragette Margaret Thompson was asked by the prison doctor in Holloway if she was a vegetarian, she put it simply: 'In here I am,' she said.

(LSE, 7JCC/O/02/086)

EMILY WILDING DAVISON KEPT PRISON FORCE-FEEDERS AT BAY USING A HAIRBRUSH

WOMEN USED EVERY TACTIC THEY COULD TO AVOID being force-fed, and many were ingenious.

In 1909 alone, Emily Wilding Davison was arrested five times. Incarcerated in Strangeways Prison, Manchester, she suffered force-feeding for the first time, a brutal experience that would stay with her for the rest of her life. Afterwards, desperate to avoid a repeat, she barricaded herself inside her cell, using bed planks, a stool, two slippers and a hairbrush to block the door. Prison staff, in an unsuccessful attempt to flush her out, inserted a hosepipe through the cell window and blasted her with icy water. It was so cold and ran so fiercely that she genuinely believed she would drown. 'The thought in my mind,' she later wrote, 'was that the moment for the sacrifice, which we have all agreed will probably be demanded, was at hand … I had no fear.'

The door was eventually broken down before the waters could cover her, and poor Emily was force-fed again. In January of 1910, she won a case against Strangeways' authorities for breaching prison regulations by using the hosepipe. The court awarded her 40 shillings in damages.

EMILY WILDING DAVISON. (LSE, 7JCC/O/02/140)

UPPER-CLASS SUFFRAGETTES RECEIVED BETTER TREATMENT

THE TREATMENT RECEIVED BY A SUFFRAGETTE IN prison was dependent on her class – as Constance Lytton, the daughter of one of the most aristocratic families in England, was to find.

Constance's father had been Viceroy of India. One of her brothers sat in the House of Lords. Another was an MP. Having been born with a serious heart condition, Constance grew up a cosseted invalid. She joined the WSPU in 1908, and nothing about her childhood could have prepared her for what was to follow. She was imprisoned four times. In 1909, finding herself in prison again, she went on hunger strike. Unlike her working-class friends, Constance was not forcibly fed. Her release was instead arranged. Her request to be treated as an ordinary inmate – that is, to share in their ill-treatment – was refused by the governor. Hearing this, she took up a needle and a piece of broken enamel from her hatpin and used it to mutilate her breast, carving the letter 'V' just above her heart. Her intention had been to write 'votes for women', a much more substantial effort which was prevented by the timely arrival of prison staff.

After her release, Constance disguised herself as a poor seamstress, Jane Warton, and got herself re-arrested in Liverpool in 1910, determined to expose the preferential treatment she received as an upper-class woman. After refusing food and drink, her time had come: she was forcibly fed, without even so much as a brief medical examination (which would have revealed her health issues). She endured another seven sessions of the torture before her mother tracked her down and had her released. Her health was already damaged by her childhood ailments. A debilitating stroke followed, and further militant activities were curtailed. She continued to fight for the cause through her writings, most notably her book *Prisons and Prisoners* (1914). She died in 1923, her death almost certainly hastened by her experiences. Her time as an active Suffragette may have been brief, but through it she succeeded in highlighting the unfairness of the prison system when it came to matters of class. She never regretted her actions, saying that she felt 'more alive' during her time as a Suffragette than at any other time in her life.

THE WSPU RAN NURSING HOMES FOR RECOVERING SUFFRAGETTES

MARION DUNLOP BECAME THE FIRST SUFFRAGE hunger striker on 1 July 1909. Her strike lasted for ninety-one hours, during which she was tempted with hearty meals. Four years later, the government introduced the Temporary Discharge for Ill-Health Act in 1913, which allowed for the early release of prisoners weakened by hunger strike. When their health recovered, they were recalled to prison again. The Temporary Discharge for Ill-Health Act, known as the Cat and Mouse Act (with the government the cat, pouncing on the suffrage 'mice'), meant prison sentences could take years to complete.

Rest homes were set up for Suffragette ex-prisoners needing somewhere to recover from the effects of hunger striking and

force-feeding. Between the spring of 1910 and 1912, a commemorative orchard was created near Bath, in the grounds of the Blathwayt family home, the site of one such home. When each of the patients, sixty-eight in total, recovered, they planted an evergreen tree or holly bush, eventually creating an arboretum. Others went to recover at the WSPU's nursing home in Pembridge Gardens, or at a private house in Campden Hill Square nicknamed 'Mouse Castle'.

The Cat and Mouse Act led many Suffragettes to go into hiding after release in order to evade re-arrest. One afternoon, when police arrived to re-arrest one Suffragette, a dozen women, all dressed in the same clothes, rushed out of the house and ran in different directions. The police, confounded, could not identify the prisoner they had come for, and she escaped. Suffragettes did not give themselves up easily to police either, frequently fleeing in disguise or by hiding inside containers such as laundry baskets. Some escapees went as far as to leave the country: at least one, Jennie Baines, succeeded in emigrating to Australia with her husband before she could be recaptured.

THE FIRST PRISONER TO BE RELEASED UNDER THE CAT AND MOUSE ACT WAS A MAN

MEN ALSO WENT ON HUNGER STRIKE AND WERE force-fed. Hugh Franklin, leader of the Men's Political Union for Women's Enfranchisement, was force-fed an extraordinary 114 times. He was the first prisoner to be released under the Cat and Mouse Act. After this ordeal, he received a letter from fourteen City of London tradesmen saying: 'We would give you and old Mother Pankhurst (the fossil-worm) 5 years Penal Servitude and then burn you both together. YOU ARE A DIRTY TYKE AND A DANGEROUS MADMAN.'

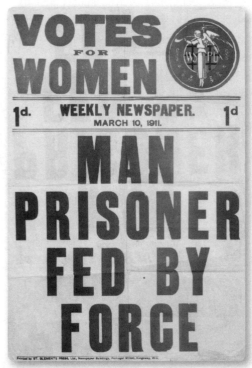

(LSE, 7HFD/A/5/09)

William Ball, a workman, was imprisoned for throwing stones. Refusing food, he was then force-fed. The prison authorities wrote to his wife, telling her that they intended to certify her husband as insane. Christabel Pankhurst took up the case – and spotted a legal loophole. She insisted that two doctors of the WSPU's choosing should examine him, informing the newspapers that if he was indeed insane then he should not have been force-fed. When William was finally released from the asylum, he claimed that he had also been subjected to electric-shock treatment while being strapped down for feeding. However, his testimony was dismissed by a disbelieving State as being the words of someone 'not strong intellectually', and 'defective in general knowledge'. A further mark held against him was his lack of education: he was illiterate.

The Men's League of the WSPU had branches in places such as London and Manchester. The men often married Suffragettes. For example, Sidney Ashman, a men's suffrage supporter, was married to a Scottish Suffragette, Anna Munro, whom he first saw speak in Reading.

SOME WOMEN WERE FORCE-FED HUNDREDS OF TIMES

KITTY MARION, A STRUGGLING VARIETY ARTISTE, WAS A member of both the Actresses' Franchise League and the WSPU.

She took part in stone-throwing and many arson attacks between 1909 and 1913. When arrested, she always went on hunger strike – and always resisted being forcibly fed. On one occasion she managed to barricade her cell door and hold out for twenty-four hours before the guards finally broke in. On another, in the early hours of the morning, she gnawed a hole in her pillow, emptied out the stuffing, broke the glass of the gas jet in her cell and, using pages from the Bible, set fire to her cell. She was already unconscious by the time she was discovered.

During her last period of imprisonment, Kitty was force-fed three times a day for five weeks and five days, which resulted in a weight loss of 2st 8lb. She endured forcible feeding no fewer than 232 times. As a further sacrifice, she was forced to give up her profession as she missed so many performances because of her frequent arrests. Her notoriety had also meant that some theatres would not book her, making work harder to come by. In 1915, as Kitty was German by birth, she was made eligible for deportation to Germany. Still suffering the after-effects of her force-feeding, mercifully Kitty was finally allowed to travel to America. Her fare was paid by a number of her Suffragette friends.

KITTY MARION. (LSE, TWL 2002 177)

THE WSPU WAS UNPOPULAR IN WALES

WOMEN ACROSS BRITAIN SUPPORTED SUFFRAGE, campaigning across the length and breadth of the British Isles, but different groups were more active than the militant groups in some areas.

In Wales, the Pankhurst's campaign against the government and to 'Keep the Liberals Out' was unpopular in a country solidly Liberal in its political leanings. Consequently, the NUWSS was more popular in South and Mid Wales. The Women's Freedom League was also very active. David Lloyd George, the target of so many militant actions, was Welsh, and his political status was something many of his fellow countrywomen and men were proud of. However, he remained a target, even in his home country. Protesters disrupted his speech at the 1912 Eisteddfod in Caernarfon and the opening of a new village hall in Llanystumdwy. After a meeting in Hale in Cheshire, as a punishment for disrupting Lloyd George's meeting, the militants were kept in the hall until they had missed their last train home. They had to walk 7 miles to the nearest Suffragette's house, where they camped out until they were able to return home the next day.

'KEEP THE LIBERALS OUT.'
(LSE, TWL.1998.62)

SUFFRAGETTES WENT ON MASS WINDOW-BREAKING EXCURSIONS

ON 1 MARCH 1912, AT 5.45 P.M., 150 WOMEN CARRYING hammers broke windows all the way along Oxford Street, Regent Street and the Strand. Scottish Suffragettes, meanwhile, smeared windows in Scotland with treacle and brown paper (to deaden the sound and reduce flying shards) before smashing them. The shards of paper left behind bore a message: votes for women. Unfortunately for the shopkeepers, many of those who had their windows smashed actually supported suffrage. London stores that sold a range of Suffragette paraphernalia were not excluded from the chaos; hammers or stones collided with their plate-glass windows also. One jeweller, hopeful of saving his windows, even stuck a notice in his shop window. It read: 'Ladies, if we had the power to grant it, you should have the vote right away. Please do not smash these windows; they are not insured.'

DAMAGE CAUSED BY SUFFRAGETTES IN 1912.
(LIBRARY OF CONGRESS, LC-DIG-GGBAIN-10220)

THE SUFFRAGETTES HELD GLOBAL CONFERENCES

WOMEN'S SUFFRAGE CAMPAIGNS TOOK PLACE ACROSS the world. There was much coming and going between suffrage movements in different countries, which sometimes carried a hint of imperialist superiority. The International Suffrage Conference, held in Budapest in 1913, was attended by 240 delegates from twenty-two countries, including Germany, the Netherlands, Sweden, Great Britain, the United States, Scandinavia, Switzerland, Italy, Russia, Belgium, Austria, South Africa and Canada.

BRITISH DELEGATION AT THE WOMEN'S INTERNATIONAL LEAGUE FOR PEACE AND FREEDOM CONFERENCE IN ZURICH, 1919. (LSE, WILPF/22/1)

Nevertheless, within national suffrage organisations there were sometimes tensions between women of different classes or races. The suffrage movement in Britain was shaped by the members' upbringing in a country with a colonial empire; when New Zealand gave women the vote in 1893, British Suffragettes struggled to come to terms with Maori women having the vote when they did not. The movement was not restricted to white women, but some of the emotive language used by Emmeline Pankhurst suggesting that privileged British women's disenfranchisement was akin to 'slavery' continues to cause offence today, especially amongst groups most affected by the evils of the slave trade. In the USA, the African-American historian and civil-rights activist W.E.B. DuBois, one of the co-founders of the NAACP (National Association for the Advancement of Colored People), suggested the demand for women's suffrage was 'a great human question ... not uninteresting or unimportant to coloured citizens of the world'. Many white women, however, did not see the situation that way and the suffrage movement, particularly in the USA, remained sadly divided by race.

QUEEN VICTORIA WAS AGAINST WOMEN'S SUFFRAGE

MANY WOMEN VEHEMENTLY OPPOSED WOMEN'S suffrage, including Queen Victoria. Intriguingly, Princess Louise, Queen Victoria's fourth daughter, was more sympathetic to the cause of women's suffrage and had connections to some of the non-militant suffragists. Other prominent anti-suffragists included Prime Minister Asquith's wife, and Virginia Woolf's mother.

Another anti-suffragist was the popular novelist Mary Ward, who wrote her books under the name Mrs Humphry Ward. In 1889 she had published *An Appeal against Women's Suffrage*, which was endorsed by 104 society women. In 1908 she founded the Anti-Suffrage League. It was an immediate success and, by 1910, the almost exclusively middle- or upper-class membership had reached 16,000 people. A further 400,000 had signed a petition against women's suffrage. The League produced pamphlets such as The Natural Right of Man to Sovereign Authority over Women and posters such as Votes for Women, NEVER! The text of the poster ran:

Men of England, your interests and those of your families and the welfare of the country are in danger. Rally to prevent it. A large number of women are demanding votes for Parliament ... Remember there are 1,300,000 more women than men in the United Kingdom and if everybody has a vote, men will be outnumbered, women will have the dominant political power – in fact, the government of the Country and the Empire will have passed from your hands to those of women ... They call it 'justice' and 'equality'. It is nothing of the kind. It is the subjection of man to woman, turning the order of nature upside down. It is contrary to common sense, to experience, and to history. Men in all ages have had to do the brunt of the world's business and ought to govern ... Play up and save your country. Save Suffragist women from themselves, and other women from Suffragists.

MRS HUMPHREY WARD. (LIBRARY OF CONGRESS, LC-DIG-GGBAIN-07427)

The Women's National Anti-Suffrage League only lasted two years before merging with the Men's National League for Opposing Women's Suffrage. The amalgamation was more of a takeover: the president of the Men's League, Lord Cromer, became president of the new National League for Opposing Women's Suffrage, with Lady Jersey initially as vice president.

EMMELINE PANKHURST DUBBED WOMEN WHO OPPOSED HER 'TRAITORS'

THERE WERE DIVISIONS IN THE WSPU. AS THE WSPU increasingly engaged in illegal activities, Christabel and Emmeline became more autocratic. This was challenged when some of the leading lights of the organisation presented a democratic constitution for consideration at the WSPU Conference in 1907 – only to see it torn up by Emmeline, who condemned its authors as traitors and conspirators, arguing division would weaken the movement. Those who opposed her left and formed their own group, the Women's Freedom League (WFL).

There were other splits in later years. The Pethick-Lawrences, who had initially bankrolled the movement (and who Christabel had lived with when she first came to London), were also thrown out of the movement after criticising Christabel's militant tactics and campaign of smashing shop windows. In 1912, Emmeline is alleged to have told the Pethick-Lawrences: 'If you do not accept Christabel's tactics, we will smash you.' The split became the subject of a cartoon in *Punch*: an image of two fashionable young women having a heated discussion in a café carried the caption 'THE SPLIT. The Budding Suffragette says: "I say Prissy (with Intensity). Are you a Peth or a Pank?"'

EMMELINE PETHICK-LAWRENCE AND CHRISTABEL PANKHURST, C. 1908–12.
(LSE, 7JCC/O/02/124)

AN EFFIGY OF A SUFFRAGETTE WAS BURNED ON BONFIRE NIGHT

AS TIME WENT ON, OPPOSITION TO THE SUFFRAGETTE movement grew vitriolic. Graphic anti-suffrage cartoons depicted Suffragettes as grotesque deranged creatures who neglected their families when campaigning for the vote, or as ugly embittered 'old maids' who would become 'thinner, dark-featured, lank or dry' if they got the vote. Their critics often implied an association between suffrage campaigning and sexual deviance. When ridicule and criticism proved to have little effect, the opposition to the Suffragettes grew even darker, with effigies of Suffragettes burned at the Lewes Bonfire night celebrations, for example.

In March 1914 the *Birmingham Gazette* published a letter from 'The Mysterious Fifty' who described how they would deal with the women involved in the militant campaigns in the city. The group took credit for vandalising the WSPU offices in John Bright Street and covering the door with a mud-like substance made by mixing black paint and acid. They threatened a programme of revenge including but not limited to personal disfigurement using acid; cutting off women's hair; ruining clothes with acid; binding and gagging; destroying suffrage literature; tarring and feathering; branding of the face; and the destruction of WSPU quarters, and any premises found harbouring women involved in suffrage militancy. The letter was signed 'We're Satisfied Prison is Useless'.

AN ANTI-SUFFRAGE
CARTOON. (LSE, TWL.2000.61)

THE FIRST SUFFRAGETTES WERE LABOUR SUPPORTERS

CAMPAIGNS FOR WOMEN'S SUFFRAGE AND THE EARLY Labour movement initially saw themselves as politically aligned. Isabella O. Ford, a member of the Leeds branch of the NUWSS and a pioneer of women's trade unionism, was one of the founders of the Independent Labour Party (ILP).

Mrs Pankhurst and Annie Kenney campaigned for the ILP's leader, Keir Hardie, who advocated that 'it is desirable that sex should cease to be a bar to the exercise of the parliamentary franchise'. Christabel Pankhurst, however, expressed growing impatience towards Labour Party MPs: 'From what I have heard,' she said, 'it is quite necessary to keep an eye on them … The further one goes the plainer one sees that men (even Labour men) think more of their own interests than of ours.' The following year, she and Emmeline resigned from the ILP, causing erstwhile supporters like Teresa Billington-Greig to resign from the WSPU in protest, saying, 'militancy has been degraded from revolution into political chicanery … It apes rebellion.'

Sylvia Pankhurst, who organised the East London Suffragettes, remained a strong supporter of the Labour Party – and was Keir Hardie's lover. She described him in the *Woman's Dreadnought* as 'the greatest human being of our time'. In 1914, as tensions grew, the East London Suffragettes' connection with the ILP and socialism caused their expulsion from the WSPU.

KEIR HARDIE. (LIBRARY OF CONGRESS, LC-DIG-GGBAIN-01224)

THE SUFFRAGETTES HAD A PATRON SAINT

SOME CAMPAIGNERS SAW THE FIGHT FOR SUFFRAGE as a holy war. The suffrage movement as a whole frequently used warrior language and iconography; Emmeline Pankhurst declared in 1909, 'Nothing but death will stop the individual soldier in the women's army from her fight for liberty.' Little wonder that Joan of Arc (who, with the 500th anniversary of her death falling in 1912, had a place in the popular imagination) was regarded as the patron saint of the movement. She was depicted on posters and in publications – and even featured in Emily Wilding Davison's funeral procession.

However, the Suffragettes' relationship with the Church itself was not always easy. When church buildings became targets for Suffragette attacks, the public was outraged. St Catherine's church in Hatcham, London, suffered an arson attack in May 1913 – and a small bomb was placed in St Paul's Cathedral. At Westminster Abbey in 1914, a nail bomb concealed in a bicycle bell exploded in front of the High Altar, damaging the Coronation Chair (then kept in the middle of the abbey). A 'huge column of smoke' flew up to the roof, and plaster poured down from it. The perpetrators were thought to have fled the scene in the confusion. A 'woman's feather boa, a guide-book and a silk bag' were found on a chair nearby. Unfortunately, two innocent ladies came briefly under suspicion and had rather an unpleasant time of it: they were booed and hissed by the crowd, and newspapers reported that 'an old woman, an itinerant vendor, made a rush at them': she had to be warded off by the police. The blast also blew 'little chips' from the Stone of Scone, and left 'the traces of [it] having been struck by bullets'. The next day a firm new rule sent many a female visitor unhappily away: 'no woman with a parcel or bag is permitted to enter'. Graffiti was also painted all over the interior of St Philip's Cathedral, Birmingham, in protest against the forced feeding of Suffragettes.

Despite these acts, some Church leaders remained appalled by the forced feeding of the suffrage prisoners, and campaigned against the harsh treatment of Suffragettes. The Church League for Women's Suffrage, founded in 1909, had grown to 103 branches and 5,080 members by 1913.

AT LAST !

CHRISTABEL PANKHURST LIVED WITH A FRENCH PRINCESS IN PARIS

IN 1912 CHRISTABEL ESCAPED TO PARIS, WHERE SHE lived for a time with her friend Princesse de Polignac, who introduced her to Parisian society.

Christabel eventually acquired her own apartment and a small Pomeranian dog. She wrote the *Votes for Women* magazine almost single-handed but, when not writing, seems to have spent most of her time shopping, visiting friends, attending theatres and concerts, and strolling with her dog on the Bois de Boulogne. Meanwhile, at home, militant Suffragettes were being arrested and force-fed. Annie Kenney, her devoted acolyte, secretly travelled every Friday to Paris to get orders from Christabel, returning on Sunday with Christabel's editorial for *Votes for Women*. In April 1913, Mary Leigh went to Paris with two other loyal supporters to tell Christabel that support was ebbing away and the movement lacked funds to support women on the run from the police. Many years later, she recalled that Christabel had 'treated me like a crazy stranger. I didn't stay long and I didn't get anywhere.' At that time WSPU organisers were paid £2 a week. Christabel received over five times that amount. Emmeline, however, refused to hear a word against Christabel, her favourite child (and the only one she had breast-fed).

EMMELINE AND CHRISTABEL IN PARIS, 1912. (LSE, 7JCC/O/02/119)

EMMELINE'S YOUNGEST DAUGHTER ADELA, WHO TOILED hard building up support for the WSPU in the North of England while also working for her teaching certificate, had rather a hard life.

She was subjected to both verbal and physical abuse at meetings on many occasions, and arrested several times, once by a burly policeman who grabbed her and dragged her away, shouting repeatedly that she should be 'smacked and set to work at the washing tubs'. Eventually she lost her temper and slapped his hand – whereupon she was promptly arrested for assault. On another occasion she was assaulted by a gang of rough youths, egged on by an older man (who shouted obscenities at her while the police stood by, refusing her requests for help). In 1912, worn down by these and other trials, she suffered a breakdown. After recovering, she unsuccessfully attempted to launch a career in horticulture. In 1914 she was sent to Australia by her mother. Emmeline provided her fare, £20, and a letter of introduction to an Australian suffragist, Vida Goldstein. Adela later married there and had five children, whom Emmeline never saw.

VOTES FOR WOMEN.

Miss ADELA PANKHURST,
Organiser, National Women's
Social and Political Union,
4, Clement's Inn, Strand, W.C.

adela Pankhurst

ADELA PANKHURST. (LSE, TWL 2002 98)

EVEN SUFFRAGE SUPPORTERS SOMETIMES OBJECTED TO WSPU TACTICS

A NUMBER OF SUFFRAGE SUPPORTERS OPPOSED THE use of militant tactics. The escalation of militant actions in 1913–14 had critics, even amongst supporters of women's suffrage. Some disassociated themselves from the more extreme activities by issuing posters and cartoons. Others took more direct action.

In 1913, the NUWSS organised the suffragist pilgrimage to London. *The Times* reported that on Saturday, 26 July, a country-wide pilgrimage 'of the law-abiding advocates of votes for women ended in a great gathering in Hyde Park, attended by some 50,000 persons'. The article suggested the proceedings 'were as much a demonstration against militancy as one in favour of woman suffrage'. Miss Margaret Robertson, a speaker at the event, stated: 'If the whole assembly were to march to Downing-street and smash every window there, they would not compel the Government to bring in a Women's Suffrage Bill.'

The Suffragettes did not suffer this criticism quietly. On the same day, *The Times* described a gathering of 15,000 'militant women and their supporters' in Trafalgar Square, which the women had held on the following day, on Sunday, 27 July. The sympathies of Miss Sylvia Pankhurst, who was later arrested, were clear: 'We have come here to hold a council of war,' she informed the crowd.

THE NATIONAL UNION OF WOMEN'S SUFFRAGE SOCIETIES PROTESTS AGAINST VIOLENCE

IT DID SO IN 1908, 1909 & 1911, & DOES SO NOW

Our Union is far the Largest, the Oldest, and has always worked for WOMEN'S SUFFRAGE by NON-PARTY & LAW-ABIDING METHODS

LOCAL SECRETARY:

NUWSS PROTESTS AGAINST VIOLENCE, C. 1912.
(LSE, TWL/1999/32/3)

115

SUFFRAGETTES ONCE THREW A HATCHET AT THE PRIME MINISTER

INITIALLY, THE BRITISH SUFFRAGETTES SEEMED KEEN to recruit Irish women to their cause. In October 1910, Emmeline Pankhurst made a speaking tour of Irish towns, including Derry and Cork. She was accompanied by Margaret Cousins, one of the founders of the Irish Women's Franchise League in 1908. By 1912 they had formed the feminist publication *Irish Citizen*. Irish militant activities that we know of included smashing the windows of the GPO Custom House and at the castle in Dublin – and indeed the first woman to be elected to the Westminster Parliament was an Irishwoman, Constance Markievicz, although as a member of Sinn Féin she did not take up her seat.

The prime minister, Herbert Henry Asquith, visited Dublin in July 1912, and was greeted by protestors from the various Irish women's suffrage groups. Two English Suffragettes in the crowd then proceeded to throw a hatchet at him, an act which horrified Irish Nationalists. This led Sylvia Pankhurst to suggest that British Suffragettes should leave the Irish Question to Irish women. By the following year, relations between the Pankhursts and Irish Suffragettes seem to have broken down. The WSPU frequently drew attention to what they perceived to be their unfair treatment by the government in comparison to the way Irish protestors were treated, which cannot have helped matters.

A few years later, in 1915, Margaret Cousins accompanied her husband when he took up a job in India, taking her experience of campaigns in Ireland to the Indian fight for social and political freedom, promoting women's education and condemning child marriages.

THE SUFFRAGETTES PROMOTED MALE ABSTINENCE

IN 1913, OLIVE HOCKIN, WHO SAT IN THE DOCK ACCUSED of setting fire to Roehampton golf course, explained that she had been attracted to the suffrage movement after becoming aware of the evils of prostitution and its deleterious effect on women's lives.

Christabel Pankhurst, in particular, suggested that women's enfranchisement would bring about a change in men's sexual morality. Christabel's tract *The Great Scourge and How to End It*, written in 1913, linked the fight for women's suffrage with struggles against venereal diseases and for moral standards to be applied equally to men and women – hence male chastity. It was hoped prostitution and sexually contracted diseases would decrease with women's enfranchisement. When the Carnegie Library in Birmingham was burned down in February 1913, destroying 1,500 books, a copy of *The Great Scourge and How to End It* was left in the rubble, with a note announcing 'To start your new library, Give Women the Vote'. For the many men who supported women's suffrage, the increasing debate about men's role in promoting social purity through abstinence outside marriage may have been uncomfortable.

CITY OF MANCHESTER.

PREVENTION OF

VENEREAL DISEASE

1. Prevention of disease is better than cure, and as regards Venereal Disease, infinitely better.
2. **The greatest protection is purity of life.**
3. But even this occasionally fails to protect from disease.
4. Self-disinfection can be easily and efficiently carried out by the individual, as shown in the leaflet "Directions to Men."
5. "Early Treatment" at an ablution Centre is really delayed disinfection. If, however, it is carried out by a skilled Attendant directly after exposure to risk of infection, it would be effective.
6. Time is the whole essence of Prevention. Therefore, immediate careful self-disinfection by the average individual is much more likely to produce satisfactory results than delayed disinfection even under skilled supervision.
7. **It is the duty of every man to safeguard the race, and to use the effectual means of disinfection advocated in the leaflet. It becomes an imperative duty to do so when there is possible risk of contamination.**
8. If, from any failure to apply the means of prevention skilfully and in time, disease should be contracted, the same means will not avail to cure, and medical aid must be obtained at the first sign of disease.

The leaflet "Directions to Men" may be obtained free by sending a stamped envelope with your address on it to

The HON. SECRETARY,
    Society for the Prevention of Venereal Disease,
        143, Harley Street, LONDON, W 1.

or by application, personally or in writing, as above, to the MEDICAL OFFICER OF HEALTH, Public Health Office, 1, Mount Street, MANCHESTER.

JAMES NIVEN,
    MEDICAL OFFICER OF HEALTH.

(LSE, 3AMS/O/120103_001)

A SUFFRAGETTE ATTACKED THE CROWN JEWELS

LEONORA COHEN, WHO (DESPITE ACTING AS ONE OF Emmeline Pankhurst's bodyguards) disagreed with her leader's attacks on private premises, declared she would undertake 'my own protest in my own way'. Rather than smash shop windows, she decided to break the glass surrounding the Crown Jewels. In February 1913 she entered the Tower of London and threw an iron bar, damaging the glass case in the Jewel Room containing the insignia of the Order of Merit and earning herself the nickname of 'the Tower Suffragette'. She was locked in the dungeon at the Tower to await the inevitable judgement of the law – but was eventually acquitted by a sympathetic jury, who failed to agree on her guilt.

Cohen later earned an OBE for her service as a Justice of the Peace, and lamented that her reputation rested on her earlier rebellious actions. 'It is curious,' she said, 'that now I am remembered for the early days of protest rather than for more than thirty years' good work as a Justice of the Peace.'

THE TOWER OF LONDON. (LIBRARY OF CONGRESS, LC-DIG-PPMSC-08566)

SYLVIA PANKHURST LED A DELEGATION TO DOWNING STREET

ON 23 JANUARY 1913, A GROUP OF TWENTY WORKING women were allowed to state their case to Lloyd George and Sir Edward Grey. It was Sylvia Pankhurst's idea, but the women were accompanied by Flora Drummond and Annie Kenney. Factory workers, teachers, fisherwomen, nurses and shop assistants were there, as were domestic servants, tailoresses and other sweated workers. They told stories of great hardship. Leonora Cohen, representing the tailoresses, told how women earned three and a half pence an hour while the men earned six and a half for exactly the same job. 'In slack time,' she went on, 'the girls go day after day and get no work given to them. A hunted look comes over their faces as they realise they are being driven onto the streets. Raise their status, Mr Lloyd George, help them to get rid of that hunted look.' Mrs King, a fisherwoman from Scotland, stated her case more bluntly: 'Give me my vote, Mr Lloyd George: I've come four hundred miles to get it and I want it before I go back.'

Despite their best efforts, and the ministers admitting they were moved by the stories they heard, they would not commit themselves to support the bill for women's suffrage.

DAVID LLOYD GEORGE.
(LIBRARY OF CONGRESS, LC-USZ62-8054)

SUFFRAGETTES HAD GUNS

ACCORDING TO SYLVIA PANKHURST'S AUTOBIOGRAPHY, older women found a novel way of supporting the militant campaigns: applying for gun licences to scare the authorities into thinking they were planning a revolution. Evelyn Morrison was one of the women issued with a gun licence, granted on 4 July 1912. She was sixty-two years old. The anxiety created by the applications for gun licences, and the resulting fear that women were planning a revolution, was perhaps given credibility by the increasing popularity of shooting as a sport for women. Indeed

one Suffragette, Miss Mary Bridson, the Honorary Secretary of the NUWSS in Bolton, even wrote articles for various magazines on big-game shooting.

The Suffragette gun fever reached its climax on 9 March 1913 in Glasgow. A meeting was held at which Mrs Pankhurst was due to speak. Tensions were running high, and the 'bodyguard' had made preparations to try to protect her from the police, who were expected to attempt to re-arrest her at the event. However, when the police tried to get onto the stage from the side, a Suffragette named Janie Allen rose from her seat on the platform and fired a pistol at the first policeman. He fell back in fright, thinking he had been mortally wounded – though in fact the cartridge was a blank. Other Suffragettes, using similar tactics, flung stones and iron balls labelled 'bombs' through windows to cause maximum alarm without real harm.

SUFFRAGETTES WERE PROLIFIC ARSONISTS

PRESTON-BORN EDITH RIGBY'S SUFFRAGETTE activities included planting a bomb in the Liverpool Corn Exchange and setting fire to Lord Leverhulme's house at Rivington Pike in 1913. 'I want to ask Sir William Lever whether he thinks his property on Rivington Pike is more valuable as one of his superfluous houses ... or as a beacon lighted to King and Country to see there are some intolerable grievances for women,' she declared from the dock.

The Suffragettes' intention, although not always successful, was to damage property alone. They withdrew from properties

if they discovered anyone in residence. In 1913 the cost of the damage by Suffragettes was estimated at between £630,000 and £750,000, not including the cost of smashed windows and the burning of letters. When these were included, the total bill for Suffragette destruction came to between £1 and £2 million. In the seven months up to the start of the war on 4 August 1914, there were 107 recorded arson attacks. Prominent targets included the Britannia Pier, Great Yarmouth. However, there is some doubt as to whether the WSPU were responsible for all the arson attacks reported: perhaps it was easier to blame them when any building was damaged or burnt. Arson campaigns were not always focused on political targets. Suffragettes set fire to buildings, including teacher-training colleges and the teahouse at Kew Gardens, where three orchid houses were also smashed and the plants exposed and torn up by the roots.

GREAT YARMOUTH PIER. (LIBRARY OF CONGRESS, LC-DIG-PPMSC-09027)

SUFFRAGETTES SOMETIMES CARRIED OUT REVENGE ATTACKS

ETHEL MOORHEAD WAS THE FIRST PRISONER TO BE forcibly fed in Scotland. She was on hunger, thirst and sleep strike by the time the doctors reached her cell. After food was forced into her, she developed double pneumonia. Her doctor stated this was due to food entering her lungs whilst being forcibly fed, but the prison authorities insisted that it was instead caused by a chill brought on by her own behaviour. After the intervention of an Edinburgh lawyer, who threatened to prosecute the prison if they tried to forcibly feed her again, she was released under the Cat and Mouse Act. She managed to avoid being recaptured until the amnesty at the start of the First World War ended the suspense.

It is likely that her best friend Francis Parker, incensed by Ethel's mistreatment, was the woman responsible for the burning down of Whitekirk church, East Lothian, in February 1914, in an act of retaliation. She was later arrested after being caught trying to burn down Robert Burns' cottage.

ROBERT BURNS' COTTAGE. (LIBRARY OF CONGRESS, LC-USZ62-112345)

WOMEN USED INGENIOUS DISGUISES TO AVOID BEING ARRESTED

ONE OF THE MOST PROLIFIC ESCAPEES WAS LILIAN Lenton. Lilian pledged to burn two buildings a week until the vote was won. She was arrested six times. Each time she went on hunger strike; despite once nearly dying while in prison (see 051), however, she remained determined to carry out her pledge.

Lilian relied on disguises to help her avoid capture. She once disguised herself as a schoolgirl, donning two plaits, a gymslip, spectacles and a panama hat to escape the police after she had been released under the Cat and Mouse Act. On another occasion, disguised as a delivery boy, she evaded arrest by climbing up a coal-delivery chute. After yet another arrest, she went on hunger and thirst strike. Once again she became seriously ill and, on her release, she was persuaded to escape to France to recover. Once she regained her strength, however, she returned to England to carry on the fight. On 5 May 1914, the *London Evening News* reported:

> She led the police a merry dance up and down the country for several weeks while she changed her disguises. Harrogate, Scarborough and Dundee were a few of the towns she visited. She also stayed in Cardiff. There she was nearly caught, but by disguising herself as an infirm old lady, with a black shawl over her head, she hobbled into the railway station and travelled to London.

A HUNGER STRIKE MEDAL. LILIAN WOULD HAVE RECEIVED HER OWN FOR HER EFFORTS. (LSE, 7JHFD/D/19)

SUFFRAGETTES TARGETED
SPORTING VENUES

077

SPORT WAS SEEN AS A PRINCIPALLY MALE PASTIME
and therefore identified as a suitable target for Suffragette activities. In Glasgow a bowling green had acid poured on the turf, as
did the green at Duthie Park golf course in Aberdeen. The Balmoral
golf course had the marker flags painted in WSPU colours by Lilias
Mitchell, who also left messages demanding 'votes for women'
and drawing attention to the forcible feeding of Suffragettes.

Blackburn Rovers' football stand; the
Stockton-on-Tees, Castle Bromwich,
Hurst Park, Ayr and Kelso Racecourse
stands; Muswell Hill Cricket Pavilion;
and Routh's Boathouse in Oxford all
experienced arson attacks.

Olive Hockin was convicted of setting
fire to the Roehampton golf pavilion
on 13 February 1913. Twenty witnesses testified at her trial. Some of
the most damning pieces of evidence
were the remains of copies of *The
Suffragette* and the *Daily Herald*, with
her name pencilled on them, which
were found at the scene of the fire.
Her plan, no doubt, had been to use
them to help get the fire going.

THE SUFFRAGETTE. COPIES OF THIS
MAGAZINE AT A CRIME SCENE LED TO ONE
SUFFRAGETTE'S ARREST. (LSE, TWL.2000.73)

126

SUFFRAGETTE ACTIVITIES AFFECTED THE STOCK EXCHANGE

FUSE BOXES FOR TELEGRAPH AND TELEPHONE WIRES were Suffragette targets.

On 11 February 1913, the *Morning Post* reported that Emmeline Pankhurst had addressed a WSPU meeting at the London Pavilion, where she was delighted to report that the Scottish Suffragettes had succeeded in severing communications between Glasgow and London for several hours the previous Saturday. Twenty-five wires were severed in the Dunlop and Kilmarnock districts, and 'votes for women' cards had been found at the site. It was timed to take place on an important day in stock-market trading to cause the most inconvenience. Not only had the overhead wires been cut, but the underground wires had also been put out of action by the fuse box being blown up.

THE LONDON STOCK EXCHANGE AT ABOUT THE TIME OF THE SUFFRAGETTES' ATTACK ON TRADING. (LIBRARY OF CONGRESS, LC-DIG-GGBAIN-03117)

SUFFRAGETTE WEAPONS INCLUDED HATPINS, STICKS AND UMBRELLAS

WOMEN FOUND EFFECTIVE WEAPONS FROM AMONG
their accessories to protect themselves from the police.

On Monday, 20 July 1913, Mrs Pankhurst attempted to attend the weekly meeting of the WSPU at the Pavilion Theatre, Piccadilly Circus. The previous Saturday night she had tricked police into arresting her 'double', and escaped the siege of her Westminster flat. Anticipating her appearance at the meeting, police officers surrounded the theatre. She arrived on foot unrecognised, but once in the hall she was identified by Inspector Riley and arrested. Suffragettes believed that inside the building their leader would be secure from the law, and so fiercely resisted her arrest by brandishing fingernails and hatpins. The electric light was switched off and they fought in the dark, resulting in a number of officers receiving black eyes and cuts to their faces. Inspector Riley was nearly throttled and walls became spattered with blood. An eyewitness described the scene: '(police) pushed Mrs Pankhurst into a room and dragged her out again and one plain-clothes officer struck a gentleman over the head and cut it open. A lady's eye was also cut open.'

Mrs Pankhurst was thrust into a taxicab destined for Holloway, where she had to be carried from the cab. So great was the concern about hatpins that, on 24 February 1914, there was discussion in Parliament about forbidding their use in public places. Mr Watt MP asked if women could be denied the vote until they had voluntarily given up wearing hatpins in public. Suffragette prisoners had already been banned from wearing the offending hatpins in one prison chapel. In protest at this ruling, Kitty Marshall fixed her hat in place with her toothbrush, to the merriment of the other prisoners.

EMMELINE BEING ARRESTED WITH SOME VIOLENCE, A REGULAR OCCURRENCE. (LSE, TWL/2009/01/25)

THERE WAS AN EMPTY CARRIAGE AT EMILY WILDING DAVISON'S FUNERAL

EMILY DIED ON 8 JUNE 1913, FOUR DAYS AFTER attempting to grab the reins of the King's horse during the Derby. Her funeral procession was a carefully choreographed visual spectacle which brought parts of London to a standstill. It was estimated that 6,000 women marched in it; a further 50,000 watched the procession.

WSPU leader Emmeline Pankhurst had been released from prison, due to ill health, just two weeks earlier. She had become increasingly frail as the arrests, hunger strikes, constant surveillance (and constant attempts to avoid re-arrest) took a huge toll on her health. Nonetheless, she decided to attend Emily's funeral. She was re-arrested as she attempted to step into the carriage to attend. Her carriage therefore joined the parade without her.

A LILY CARRIED AT EMILY'S FUNERAL. (LIBRARY OF CONGRESS, 7EWD/M/28)

SUFFRAGETTES USED JIU-JITSU

EMMELINE BECAME PARTICULARLY SKILLED AT evading the police, only to pop up again at a public meeting, often surrounded by a bodyguard of Suffragettes. Led by Gertrude Harding, the bodyguard was formed in 1913. The women carried Indian clubs hidden inside their skirts. They had learned self-defence and martial arts such as jiu-jitsu in order to better protect Mrs Pankhurst, who was becoming increasingly frail from her repeated hunger strikes and was in constant danger of being re-arrested under the Cat and Mouse Act. Gertrude Harding later explained:

> All volunteers had to be carefully selected. They must be completely trust-worthy, in good physical shape and be ready at a moment's notice to do battle with the police in defence of Mrs Pankhurst. Scotland Yard did their best to introduce spies into our ranks so that they could learn what the women were armed with.

Thirty in number, the group took instruction from Edith Garrud, who – despite being only 4ft 11in tall – was the first British female jiu-jitsu expert. Meeting up for training proved difficult, as the bodyguard had to constantly change their venues to avoid the police, who had them under near-constant surveillance. Several of the bodyguard were injured trying to defend their leader, as they were heavily outnumbered by the police at every event.

SUFFRAGETTES BATONED BY POLICE

Evening News 6.30

(LSE, TWL.1999.43)

SUFFRAGETTES WERE SECRETLY PHOTOGRAPHED IN PRISON

HIDDEN CAMERAS OFTEN OBSERVED PRISONERS taking exercise in the prison yard, and police surveillance of the Suffragettes often continued when they were released.

Police and prison authorities developed quite sophisticated methods of taking the photos – although once prisoners discovered they were being photographed, they used disruptive tactics such as turning their backs to wherever they thought the camera might be or pulling faces at the camera. Plain-clothed policemen also infiltrated crowds at meetings and used hidden devices (such as a camera inside a top hat, with a tiny aperture in the front) to photograph those they saw as troublemakers.

It was also possible to 'doctor' photos. In one original photograph, of Suffragette Evelyn Manesta, a policeman's arm had been locked in a stranglehold around her neck; in the published version, however, the arm has been disguised to look as though Evelyn is wearing a scarf around her neck.

CHRISTABEL AND EMMELINE SURROUNDED BY POLICE, C. 1910. (LSE. 7JCC/O/02/120)

SUFFRAGETTES WERE DRUGGED IN PRISON

MIND-ALTERING DRUGS WERE USED ON SUFFRAGETTE prisoners. For example, there is evidence that, by 1913, Suffragette prisoners were being drugged with bromide medicines to make force-feeding easier.

Mary Richardson and Rachel Peace, who were arrested for attempting to burn down Hampton Mansions, having both been arrested several times before, were allegedly drugged before they were force-fed. However, the Home Secretary, Reginald McKenna, denied this, and files on their cases were later destroyed. By June 1914, McKenna was considering having Suffragettes declared criminally insane, announcing that he believed that 'the indignity of being sent to Broadmoor would bring them to their senses'.

Decisions were sometimes made to forcibly feed Suffragettes as a punishment for their habitual lawbreaking. Force-feeding could take place through the mouth or the nose, but other crueller possibilities were also used: for example, Fanny Parker was force-fed through both her vagina and rectum, again suggesting that forcible feeding was being used as punishment and not as treatment.

Even women who were not strictly prisoners were force-fed: in May 1914, Grace Roe was forcibly fed whilst she was on remand, contrary to regulations, as she was yet to be found guilty of any charge.

BLANDFORD FORCIBLE-FEEDING TUBE. (SCIENCE MUSEUM, LONDON, WELLCOME IMAGES)

THE WOMAN WHO ATTACKED THE ROKEBY VENUS WAS KNOWN AS 'SLASHER MARY'

MARY RICHARDSON, 'SLASHER MARY', WHO ATTACKED Velázquez's painting The Rokeby Venus at the National Gallery in 1914, made the most famous assault on an artwork. However, she was only one of many such protestors.

In the same year, Bertha Ryland used a meat cleaver to damage a painting in Birmingham Art Gallery and Museum, after which the gallery was closed for several weeks. When she was apprehended after her attack on the painting, by a well-known eighteenth-century artist George Romney, a note was discovered in her pocket book which read, 'I deliberately attacked this work of art as a protest against the Government's criminal injustice in deny-ing women the vote, and also against the Government's brutal injustice in imprisoning, forcibly feeding, and drugging suffragist militants, while allowing Ulster militants to go free.'

Fourteen paintings had already been damaged in Manchester Art Gallery the year before. In Edinburgh, Maude Evans slashed a portrait of the King in full naval uniform, held at Royal Scottish Academies, with a hatchet. Her court appearance was greeted by loud applause by a number of Suffragettes in the crowd, but the court was less impressed: she received a three-month sentence for her efforts in July 1914. At the British Museum a glass case, holding a mummy, was smashed. Anxious to preserve their col-lections, the National Gallery, the Tate Gallery and the Wallace Collection closed to the general public, leading one woman report-edly to complain at not being able to see the Wallace Collection 'because of those horrible Suffragettes'.

THE NATIONAL GALLERY AT THE TURN OF THE CENTURY.
(LIBRARY OF CONGRESS, LC-DIG-PPMSC-08573)

The press were becoming increasingly antagonistic towards the Suffragettes, the *London Evening Standard* on 9 June 1914 producing a billboard which simply read, 'let them starve'. On 12 June 1914 a suffrage meeting held at the home of Miss Winterbourne in Balham was attacked by an angry mob. The following month, on 16 July, the last Suffragette rally of peacetime was held at Holland Park Skating Rink.

THE WSPU SUSPENDED THEIR CAMPAIGN FOR SUFFRAGE TO HELP WIN THE FIRST WORLD WAR

FOR MANY SUFFRAGETTES, THE OUTBREAK OF THE First World War on 4 August 1914 was challenging.

Emmeline and Christabel Pankhurst immediately announced that all agitation by the WSPU would cease. Militant campaigns were suspended with immediate effect, and the organisation instead offered its support to the government. This decision was not wholly popular, and in the short term had some unintended consequences for women working for the organisation: Eunice Murray, who organised for the Women's Freedom League (WLF) in Scotland, noted in her diary that the confusion surrounding the Pankhursts' sudden announcement meant that many women who worked as organisers for the WSPU were left stranded around the country, many miles from home. To make matters worse, the WSPU, who had been paying their wages, now suddenly stopped. A lot of these women were forced to borrow money for the train fare home from sympathetic suffragists in the WFL, which was one of the only organisations, with the United Suffragists, to continue a national political campaign for the vote during wartime.

Some women ceased their suffrage campaigning and undertook instead a wide range of recruitment activities – but many others did not. Many, like Emmeline's daughter Sylvia in the East End, focused their efforts initially on charitable and welfare work. Other Suffragettes, many of whom were also pacifists, joined the campaign against war itself. They found the introduction of conscription for men in 1916 particularly difficult.

(LIBRARY OF CONGRESS, LC-USZC4-10915)

SOME SUFFRAGETTES TOOK AN ACTIVE ROLE IN THE FIRST WORLD WAR

SUFFRAGETTES SET UP THE WOMEN'S VOLUNTEER Reserve (WVR). Suffragette Evelina Haverfield, also keen to help women serve the war effort, set up the Women's Emergency Corps in 1914. The organisation sought to prepare women for a possible German invasion, a letter to the *Worcester Herald* explaining they intended to become 'a disciplined body of women to be used in emergency for home defence ... [and] also to prevent the indiscriminate use of firearms by untrained women'.

The group developed into the Women's Voluntary Reserve, who enrolled motorists, motorcyclists and aviators, and learnt skills such as signalling, first aid and field cooking. There was some reticence about them due to their somewhat military demeanor, the women drilling, marching and wearing khaki uniform, which members had to purchase at a cost of £2. The membership came from more affluent women and developed to undertake a range of voluntary work, including cooking and running canteens; they played a role as interpreters, as well as caring for mothers and babies, collecting and distributing clothes and helping with transportation. Amongst other duties, they were among the volunteers who helped to clear snow from the streets of Wolverhampton during a heavy deluge in 1916.

The First Rifle Practice of the Women's Reserve Corps

Messenger: The Major wants to know will you please excuse him from reviewing the practice to-day. He doesn't feel strong enough

(LIBRARY OF CONGRESS, LC-USZC2-1200)

ENGLISH AND GERMAN SUFFRAGETTES MET AT A PEACE CONFERENCE IN 1915

SUFFRAGETTES ATTENDED A PEACE CONFERENCE with German women in the Hague in 1915. Chrystal Macmillan, an executive member of the National Union of Women's Suffrage Societies (NUWSS), helped organise this International Congress of Women. It took place in April 1915 and was attended by over 1,200 women from twelve countries, including Germany, Britain, the USA and France. They gathered at the invitation of the Dutch suffrage organisation led by Alletta Jacobs who, in her opening address, explained:

With mourning hearts we stand united here. We grieve for many brave young men who have lost their lives on the battlefield before attaining their full manhood; we mourn with the poor mothers bereft of their sons; with the thousands of young widows and fatherless children, and we feel that we can no longer endure in this twentieth century of civilisation that government should tolerate brute force as the only solution of international disputes.

Over three days, the congress worked out what they considered an alternative, non-violent form of conflict resolution, calling for a process of continuous mediation to be implemented until peace could be restored. The congress also marked the foundation of the Women's International League for Peace and Freedom. Following this conference, Rosika Schwimmer, who had taken a leading role in winning the vote for Hungarian women, travelled with others throughout Europe and North America to promote the cause of neutral mediation and organise women in an attempt to stop the hostilities.

(LSE, WILPF/2011/18)

EMMELINE PANKHURST ADOPTED WAR BABIES

EMMELINE AND CHRISTABEL PANKHURST BECAME vehemently patriotic as the war rolled on. Christabel changed the name of her newspaper to *Britannia* and, with her mother, threw herself into supporting the war and encouraging men to enlist. In 1915, Emmeline became convinced that thousands of women had given birth to illegitimate children after being abandoned by men who had gone to war. She decided the WSPU should adopt fifty war babies. It later transpired that there was no great surge in illegitimate births and, as there was little response from the membership, the idea was largely dropped, although Emmeline herself adopted four three-year-old girls, whose care was handed over to a nurse.

That same year, following a meeting with Lloyd George, Emmeline was given £4,000 towards the cost of organising the Call to Women March on 17 July 1915. An estimated 30,000 women took part. As well as marching bands, there were banners proclaiming 'We Demand the Right to Serve'; purple, white and green decorations were replaced by red, white and blue. In many other ways it was reminiscent of a WSPU march and harked back to the heyday of their success. Massive crowds turned out to see the women march past – but now, in wartime, they were cheered rather than jeered.

Emmeline and Christabel Pankhurst's support for the war did not wane. Christabel had perhaps the strongest views, supporting the giving of white feathers (a symbol of cowardice) to encourage young men not in uniform to enlist. She considered nothing

EMMELINE FEEDING A BABY. (LSE, 7JCC/O/02/099)

but the complete destruction of Germany to be acceptable as an end to the hostilities. Death she considered preferable to living under German rule. Even though her sister Sylvia was a pacifist, she wrote in 1917: 'I consider the Pacifists a disease. They are a disease to which old nations seem to become subject. They are a disease which comes of over-prosperity, and of false security.'

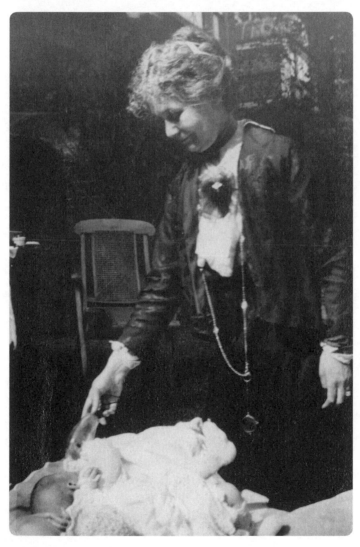

SUFFRAGETTES RAN A TOY FACTORY

AS THE WAR GROUND ON, MANY SUFFRAGETTES focused on welfare work, as wartime conditions exacerbated concerns about working-class women's health and well-being. The Women's Freedom League, the NUWSS and Sylvia Pankhurst's East London Suffragettes engaged in a range of work. They organised restaurants to feed the poorer classes, ran a clinic for mothers and children, launched a communal nursery, and helped women with the financial struggles brought about when men enlisted in the armed forces. In London a public house named The Gunmakers' Arms was acquired. Re-named The Mothers' Arms, the women ran the establishment as a clinic and crèche. They also set up a toy factory providing work for women, as before the war many toys had been imported from Germany and were therefore no longer available. The WFL also set up vegetarian restaurants in numerous parts of the country, whilst the NUWSS provided work for 2,000 women in forty workshops – including the Women's Welding School, where female students were taught oxy-acetylene welding!

However, many women who campaigned for the suffrage were also committed peace campaigners – including (unlike their mother and sister) Adela and Sylvia Pankhurst. Sylvia strongly opposed conscription, and published a number of anti-war articles in her journal, the *Woman's Dreadnought*, an attitude which led to a police raid on the Workers Suffrage Federation in East London on 3 August 1917. Sylvia was arrested and imprisoned for five months for sedition. She was not the only woman who opposed conscription, but she was one of the few whose activities gained her the attentions of the Secret Service.

(LSE, 324.62306094215 EAS AND 324.62306094215 EAS)

BABY WEIGHING IN BROMLEY.

A PAIR OF BOOTS.

BLACK BOYS.

MONKEYS.

OUR POPLAR RESTAURANT, 20 RAILWAY STREET.

IN THE NORMAN ROAD NURSERY.

On July 12th, a procession marched from Bow to Canning Town Public Hall, where a great meeting was held, at which many of the overseas visitors were present.

After this it seemed that holidays and steady propaganda work should be continued through the summer with a view to more effective militant action when Parliament met for the autumn session. The "No Rent" strike for the vote was the big achievement, towards which it seemed advisable to work.

The Declaration of War.

But our plans were overturned by the declaration of War on August 4th. As soon as that happened the E.L.F.S. Committee was called together, and it was decided that the Federation must take an actively vigilant part in striving to protect the women during the International crisis in which it was certain that they must suffer terribly in any event.

Food and Rent.

The food question engaged our immediate attention, for prices at once rose enormously, and even at the enhanced prices, many poor housewives were unable to buy because of the panic buying by richer people.

The E.L.F.S. at once demanded that the Government should control the supply of food, and that the Moratorium should be extended to cover rent.

The question of immediately proclaiming the "No Rent" strike, in order to secure this and to win votes for women, was considered by a general meeting, but it was decided that the time was inopportune, as in the meantime prices had been reduced considerably and it had been demonstrated that there was no immediate danger of a shortage of food. The Emergency Courts Acts, which afforded some protection against eviction had, also been passed.

As it was held, however, that complete Government control of the food supply was still necessary, a deputation from the Federation waited upon the President of the Board of Trade on September 2nd, and demanded that—

During the War the food supply shall be controlled by the Government in the interests of all the people, and that working women shall be placed on all Committees for fixing food prices.

The deputation supplied Mr. Runciman with a number of family budgets, showing great hardships still being suffered by poor women, to whom it is barely possible to make ends meet at the best of times.

Public Work for the Unemployed.

As soon as War broke out the E.L.F.S. also demanded that working men and women threatened of employment by the War should be provided with work at Trade Union rates by the Government, pointing out that agriculture and horticulture, food preserving, cattle rearing, and dairying, were all rendered doubly important because of the War, and that for the preservation of the coming generation, improvements in housing and sanitation were urgently overdue.

The Federation also demanded that women should be paid a minimum wage of not less than 5d. an hour, or £1 a week, on all work subsidised by public funds, or when employed by Government contractors.

Military and Naval Pensions and Separation Allowances.

The Federation also demanded that Military and Naval Pensions and Separation allowances shall be paid as a right, not as a charity, at the rate of £1 a week for an adult, and 5s. a week for each child. The Federation has also emphatically protested against the police supervision of soldiers' wives and mothers.

More Deputations.

To put forward these views, deputations from the E.L.F.S. waited upon the War Office and the Committee for London. A petition to the Queen, calling for the minimum wage of 5d. an hour, or £1 a week, above referred to, was drafted on behalf of the E.L.F.S. and signed by a number of representative men and women. The

ELEANOR RATHBONE ADDRESSING A NATIONAL UNION OF WOMEN'S SUFFRAGE SOCIETIES MEETING IN EDINBURGH AFTER THE WAR; MILLICENT GARRETT FAWCETT IS ON HER RIGHT. (LSE, TWL 2009 02 138)

SUFFRAGETTES RAN A WAR HOSPITAL IN SERBIA

THE NATIONAL UNION OF WOMEN'S SUFFRAGE RAISED and equipped women's ambulance corps and hospital units to send to Serbia during the First World War. In addition, the Scottish Women's Hospital Unit supplied nurses, doctors, cooks and orderlies to units in Corsica, France, Malta, Romania, Russia, Salonika and Serbia. On 10 November 1915, Dr Alice Hutchinson and thirty members of the 2nd Scottish Women's Hospital Unit were fighting to save lives in a hospital in Vranyaschka, Serbia. Under siege by the Austrian army, the Serbians could fight no longer and were forced to retreat, leaving the town – and the Suffragettes – undefended. When they occupied the hospital, the Austrians demanded Austrian cholera patients should be nursed. Hutchinson and her unit refused, insisting they would only aid wounded Serbian prisoners.

Dr Hutchinson's unit were sent to Kevavara in Southern Hungary, where they were treated as little more than common soldiers: twenty-two women slept on straw in rooms built for nine. Dr Hutchinson demanded under the Geneva Convention that they should be treated as members of the Red Cross. The Austrian commander countered that England had torn the Convention to shreds. For two months they endured this hardship. On 16 December 1915, Hutchinson wrote: 'I dread the journey home, especially if it lies through Germany. I feel in [German soldiers] an innate boorishness and brutality, and I realise, as I never did before, the disaster it would be to the whole world if Germany is finally victorious.'

On 28 January 1916, Hutchinson's unit were finally released, facing a nightmarish seven-week trek from Krushevatz back to London. They endured torrential rain and slept in the open air before finally returning safely home, their ordeal finally over.

A SUFFRAGETTE WAS ACCUSED OF TRYING TO POISON THE PRIME MINISTER

IN 1917, SUFFRAGE CAMPAIGNER (AND SUPPORTER OF conscientious objectors, many of whom she hid in her home) Alice Wheeldon was convicted of conspiracy to poison the Prime Minister Lloyd George and Labour MP Arthur Henderson.

Her daughter Winifred and her son-in-law, Alfred Mason, a chemist, were also convicted of conspiracy to murder. Alice Wheeldon's passage from relative obscurity to a trial at the Old Bailey began when an MI5 agent, tasked with uncovering a suspected treasonable plot in Derby, was planted in her home. Controversy still surrounds the evidence presented at her trial, which many believe to have been fabricated. Previous verbal attacks on Lloyd George by the defendant did not help her case, nor did her assertion that Suffragettes had indeed previously planned to kill Lloyd George (something Emmeline Pankhurst attended the court to deny). Her defence was that the poison she was charged with intending to administer was instead intended to destroy dogs guarding an internment camp for conscientious objectors in London. It was rejected: the camp, it appeared, did not have guard dogs. She was sentenced to ten years in prison, but released on licence in December 1917. She died within two years. Her family became ardent Communists, and indeed her son (who was later executed during a Stalinist purge in Russia) draped a red flag over her coffin at her funeral.

ARTHUR HENDERSON.
(LIBRARY OF CONGRESS, LC-DIG-GGBAIN-19213)

SOME OF THE FIRST FEMALE POLICE OFFICERS WERE SUFFRAGETTES

MILITANT SUFFRAGETTES WERE AT THE FOREFRONT of the new Women's Police Service. A number of Suffragettes, including Nina Boyle of the WFL, became Women Police Volunteers (WPV) in wartime, a group set up to assist women suffering from so-called 'khaki fever' (i.e. excitement at the presence of soldiers, which contemporaries felt led young women to behave 'immodestly'). They also had a more serious role: to protect women from the unsolicited advances of men in uniform. Anxiety over the best ways to protect women was such that, at one secondary school in Bradford, it was considered 'necessary for teachers to accompany girl scholars to and from the railway station in order to protect them from molestation'.

The WPV often monitored (and attempted to control) working-class women's behaviour around factories, munition hostels and barracks. Curfews tried to prevent young women engaging in 'inappropriate' relationships with soldiers. There were more than 2,000 of these uniformed women officers. Each wore a black, rather masculine jacket, trousers and long, black, leather boots. Armed with only a flashlight and a whistle, these women attempted to prevent acts of immorality. The activities of the WPV provided an opportunity for women to press the case for a female police force, though little progress was made with this until the Second World War.

093 CHRISTABEL PANKHURST STOOD AS AN MP FOR HER OWN POLITICAL PARTY

CHRISTABEL AND HER MOTHER EMMELINE FORMED THE Women's Party in 1917, when it became clear that women would be able to participate in a post-war election. The following year she stood as the Women's Party candidate for Smethwick in the December General Election. Christabel had support from Lloyd George and the Conservative candidate, who agreed to stand down in order to give her a clear run at this Midlands seat. However, despite poster campaigns, rallies, meetings, as well as a fleet of decorated cars and bicycles touring the streets sharing her message, Christabel was narrowly defeated. The Labour Party candidate, John Davison, gained 9,389 votes to Christabel's 8,614, taking the seat. Christabel became a religious evangelist. She took no further part in politics and moved to America.

Emmeline, meanwhile, became a Conservative. In 1926, horrified by Bolshevism, she joined the Conservative Party and was adopted as Conservative candidate for Parliament in the constituency of Whitechapel and St Georges. However, revelations about Sylvia (who had given birth to an illegitimate son), combined with failing physical and emotional health, ended Emmeline's political ambitions. She died on 14 June 1928. Mercifully, however, Emmeline Pankhurst lived long enough to see the Equal Representation Bill introduced to the House of Commons.

EMMELINE AND CHRISTABEL HIDING FROM THE POLICE ON A ROOF AT CLEMENTS INN IN 1908. (LSE, 7JCC/O/02/121)

THE FIRST WOMEN ELECTED AS AN MP WAS IN PRISON WHEN SHE WON

WHEN, IN 1918, WOMEN WERE FINALLY ALLOWED TO stand for election as MPs, seventeen women put themselves forward. All but one of them were defeated.

Sinn Féin member Constance Markievicz became the first woman to be elected to the British Parliament despite being at the time interned in Holloway Prison. Constance Markievicz was a feminist, socialist and artist, and the most well known of the 200 women who took part in the Easter Rising against British imperial rule that occurred in Dublin on Easter Monday, 1916. As one of the leaders of the uprising she was court-martialled and sentenced to be shot, but as a woman Constance's life was spared. In March 1919 Constance Markievicz was released from prison; like other members of Sinn Féin, she did not take up her seat in the House of Commons. However, she did visit to see her name over a peg in the cloakroom. She regarded the operation of parliamentary politics with some suspicion, having only a year before her election remarked in a letter to her sister: 'I don't think Parliaments are much use … All authority in a country always seems to get into the hands of a clique and permanent officials.'

'A PRISONER'S BREAKFAST', JUST ONE OF THE WAYS SUFFRAGETTES CELEBRATED WHEN SUFFRAGE PRISONERS WERE RELEASED FROM HOLLOWAY. (LSE, 7JCC/O/02/043)

SOME SUFFRAGETTES BECAME FASCISTS

SOPHIA ALLEN WAS JAILED THREE TIMES FOR HER militant Suffragette activities. She went on hunger strike during her time in prison, became a policewoman during the First World War – and then became a strong supporter of Hitler, Oswald Mosley and Fascism in the inter-war years.

In this political allegiance she was joined by Mary Richardson, the woman who had slashed the Rokeby Venus (and been imprisoned nine times in support of women's right to the vote). Richardson wrote: 'I was first attracted to the Blackshirts because I saw in them the courage, the action, the loyalty, the gift of service and the ability to serve which I had known in the Suffragette movement.' Mary quickly rose to prominence and became, for a while, the chief women's organiser of the British Union of Fascists. She left after two years, disillusionment with their policies towards women having set in.

OSWALD AND LADY CYNTHIA MOSLEY. (LIBRARY OF CONGRESS, LC-DIG-GGBAIN-38928)

MANY SUFFRAGETTES CARRIED CAMPAIGN SCARS FOR THE REST OF THEIR LIVES

THERE WERE LONG-TERM CONSEQUENCES FOR women who had been Suffragettes. In 1918 Parliament granted a legal pardon to Suffragettes with outstanding prison sentences, but for some women there were long-term health consequences from their involvement in militant activities. Many spoke, later in life, about the ongoing stomach problems caused by their time in prison and by the force-feeding they there endured. For others, the emotional and psychological consequences of their activities were the strongest legacy.

Hannah Mitchell had been a volunteer and a paid organiser for the WSPU. At the same time she kept her family, managing on very little money. She travelled to meetings in many out-of-the-way places, and frequently addressed hostile crowds. Eventually, worn down by the extreme stresses of such a life, she had a severe breakdown. She recovered, but found that she had lost her nerve. In the years to come, attending any public meeting was difficult: suffering from what we might now recognise as Post Traumatic Stress Disorder, she found that she shook uncontrollably when attending any public gathering.

For another Suffragette, Rachel Peace, the force-feeding (and also possibly the drugs she was given) had a devastating effect upon her health. She was a working-class woman, an embroideress by trade, who had already had several nervous breakdowns before being imprisoned. This did not prevent her from hunger striking but, after being force-fed three times daily, she wrote: 'I fear I shall be mentally affected ... old distressing symptoms have

EMMELINE RECOVERING FROM ONE OF THE SPELLS OF IMPRISONMENT, HERE IN 1913, THAT RUINED HER HEALTH. (LSE, 7JCC/O/02/09)

re-appeared. I have frightful dreams and am struggling with mad people half the night.' She did indeed 'lose her reason', spending the rest of her life in and out of asylums. Lady Constance Lytton paid her asylum bills for the rest of her life (an example of the solidarity and sense of sisterhood these women felt for each other, despite coming from diametrically opposite ends of the social scale).

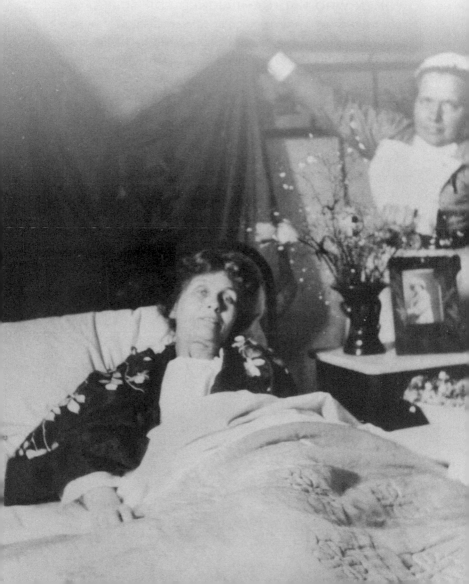

THE WOMEN'S INSTITUTE FOUNDERS INCLUDED SUFFRAGETTES

WOMEN WHO HAD CAMPAIGNED FOR SUFFRAGE became involved in a wide range of different political organisations after the war. Some, like Edith Rigby and Isabel Margesson, both active Suffragette campaigners, became leading lights in the Women's Institute Movement.

The National Federation of Women's Institute's finances were in the capable hands of Mrs Auerbach, who had also been treasurer of the National Union of Women's Suffrage Societies. The Women's Institute adopted the WSPU's purple, white and green colour scheme, as well as the suffrage hymn Jerusalem. In the 1930s, their AGM became known as the Countrywomen's Parliament. Other women's groups also had Suffragette founder members. Catherine Blair was a founder of the Scottish Women's Rural Institutes; she had been active in the WSPU, chairing meetings, writing to the press and providing rest and refuge for Suffragette prisoners. She was joined in the Rural Institutes by Nannie Brown, a member of the Women's Freedom League. With five other women, Nannie once walked 400 miles, from Edinburgh to London, collecting signatures in support of women's suffrage.

HM QUEEN ELIZABETH VISITING A WI CANNING UNIT AT READING IN AUGUST 1942.

(LSE, 5FWI/B/2/2/02/026)

SYLVIA PANKHURST DIED IN ETHIOPIA

THE RELATIONSHIPS IN THE PANKHURST FAMILY became rather strained in later years. The greatest strain arrived when Emmeline's daughter Sylvia, who objected to marriage as an institution, had a child with her partner Silvio out of wedlock. Mary Gordon, Emmeline's adopted daughter, wrote that Emmeline refused to speak to her afterwards: on hearing the news, she reportedly put down her teacup and walked out of the room, leaving Sylvia in tears. She could never forgive Sylvia for becoming an unmarried mother at the age of forty-five, nor for her left-wing politics and pacifist beliefs. Sylvia and Christabel didn't speak for over forty years. Then Sylvia suffered a serious heart attack, and Christabel wrote to her. They corresponded until a few months before Christabel died. They stuck to safe topics and obviously still disagreed about politics and religion but wrote about their shared love for their father. Interestingly, they made little mention of their mother.

Sylvia was really the child to carry on the family's radical traditions. An internationalist and socialist, she supported the Russian Revolution and played a role in the founding of the Communist Party, working with Dora Montefiore and Helen Crawford in the interwar years. She vehemently resisted Fascism and imperialism, and opposed Mussolini's invasion of Abyssinia (Ethiopia) in the 1930s. She actively fought for Ethiopian self-determination – and in fact, she died there, in Addis Ababa, in self-imposed exile, in 1960.

SYLVIA WITH A CHILD, POSSIBLY HER OWN. (LSE, 7JCC/0/02/127)

A SPECIAL CAR WAS PRODUCED TO CELEBRATE THE SUFFRAGETTES

ONCE THE VOTE WAS WON, THE WSPU AND THE Pankhursts were heralded from the rooftops. In Scotland, the planting of the Glasgow Oak commemorated Suffragette activities; in England, a campaign led to a statue of Emmeline Pankhurst opposite the Palace of Westminster, unveiled by Prime Minister Stanley Baldwin on 6 March 1930. (However, the House of Commons on several occasions voted against building a memorial to Sylvia Pankhurst: her opposition to the war and left-wing politics arguably precluded her, and many others, from a central place in national narratives of suffrage history.)

More unusual tributes to the suffrage struggles included the Galloway car. Dorothée Pullinger, manager of Galloway Motors factory in Tongland, near Kirkcudbright, adopted the Suffragette purple, white and green colours for the vehicle – which was described as 'a car built by ladies, for those of their own sex'. It was smaller and lighter than other vehicles, with a higher seat and a smaller steering wheel, all designed with women drivers in mind. Galloway Motors actually won the 1924 Scottish Six Day Trials in a Galloway. Dorothée entered in the race herself. Pullinger, a pioneer, began an engineering college at Galloway. Apprenticeships for women lasted two years less than those for men, as it was believed that women could learn faster than men.

UNVEILING THE STATUE TO EMMELINE PANKHURST.
(LSE, 7JCC/O/02/156)

THE FIRST ENGLISHWOMAN TO BECOME AN MP OPPOSED AUSTERITY

THE FIRST ENGLISH-BORN FEMALE MP WAS MARGARET (Maggie) Wintringham. She was elected in September 1921 when her husband, who was Liberal MP for Louth (Lincolnshire), suddenly died. Margaret was nominated to succeed him, though still in mourning. She apparently agreed to stand on the condition that she did not have to make public speeches during the campaign. Instead, she attended meetings where others, including her two sisters, spoke on her behalf. It seems that the party grandees felt such an arrangement would elicit public support – and it did, for she retained her seat for three years. When, in 1923, Wintringham finally spoke up in the House of Commons, she expressed her concern that the proposed Housing Bill would not lead to houses being built in rural areas. She also critiqued the austerity measures, which would result in three-bedroom houses being reduced to 850 square feet, with one of the children's bedrooms being just 6ft by 6ft 10in. As she explained to the House:

> I visualised that room in my mind, and I compared it with the Table in front of the Treasury bench, and afterwards I was interested to go down and measure the Table. I found that the smallest bedroom would be half-a-foot less in length than the Table. I ask the Minister, how would it be possible to use such a room as a bedroom for the accommodation of two girls or two boys?

THE TABLE WHICH MAGGIE USED TO REJECT AUSTERITY MEASURES. (LIBRARY OF CONGRESS, LC-USZ62-9720)

'EVERY WOMAN IS A CHANCELLOR OF THE EXCHEQUER'

SUFFRAGE CAMPAIGNERS HAD ARGUED THAT, AS housewives, women had a role to play in national government's housekeeping. When women got the vote, all political parties attempted to appeal to women voters in a similar way. For example, the Conservative leader Stanley Baldwin explained his unwillingness to reduce sugar duty in 1923 by addressing women as 'Sister Chancellors of the Exchequer'. 'Every woman is a Chancellor of the Exchequer in her own right as a housewife,' he declared. 'I am, as Chancellor of the Exchequer, the housewife of the nation. Women can realise my task if they imagine themselves living in [a] house which is mortgaged up to the hilt.'

Yet, 100 years later, no woman has yet been appointed to the office of Chancellor of Exchequer in Britain – and the number of female MPs remains dire. As of the time of writing, only 469 women have been elected to be MPs since 1918. From the early days it was a struggle to get women selected or elected. At the 2017 General Election, 218 women were elected as MPs (32 per cent of all seats, a record high); prior to 1987, women had never made up more than 5 per cent of the MPs in British Parliament. Shockingly, only forty-three women have ever been appointed to serve as Cabinet ministers.

STANLEY BALDWIN WITH HIS WIFE AND DAUGHTER.
(LSE, LC-DIG-GGBAIN-35430)

FURTHER READING

THIS BOOK DRAWS UPON A WIDE RANGE OF scholarship of the suffrage movement. We hope it will encourage you to read further and the list below is offered as a starting point.

Atkinson, Diane. *The Suffragettes in Pictures*. Sutton Publishing Limited, 1996.

Bartley, Paula. *Votes for Women*. Hodder and Stoughton, 1998.

Cowman, Krista. *Women of the Right Spirit: Paid Organisers of the Women's Social and Political Union (WSPU)*, 1904–18. Manchester University Press, 2007.

Crawford, Elizabeth. *The Women's Suffrage Movement: A Reference Guide 1866–1928*. Routledge, 2003.

Hawksley, Lucinda. *March, Women, March*. Andre Deutsch, 2013.

Liddington, Jill. *Rebel Girls: Their Fight for the Vote*. Virago Press, 2006.

Liddington, Jill. *Vanishing the Vote: Suffrage, Citizenship, and the Battle for the Census*. Manchester University Press, 2014.

Marlow, Joyce (ed.). *Votes for Women: The Virago Book of Suffragettes*. Virago Press, 2001.

Phillips, Melanie. *The Ascent of Woman: A History of the Suffragette Movement and the Ideas Behind It*. Abacus, 2004.

Purvis, June. *Emmeline Pankhurst: A Biography*. Routledge, 2003.